Values and Faith

Activities for Family and Church Groups

Roland S. Larson and Doris E. Larson

Youth and Family Institute of Augsburg College

© 1998 **Youth and Family Institute of Augsburg College**
Campus Box 70
2211 Riverside Avenue
Minneapolis, MN 55454-1351

call: 612-330-1624
fax: 612-330-1595
email: ayfi@augsburg.edu
web: http://www.augsburg.edu/ayfi/ayfi.html

ISBN   1-889407-24-0

Printed in the United States of America

Acknowledgments

Many, many persons have been a part of this book in one way or another. The cliché is true — there are too many to mention. But a number of people have been especially influential or helpful in this venture.

Our work with Howie and Barb Glaser-Kirschenbaum, Merrill Harmin, Sid Simon, Thomas Gordon, and Ralph Jones helped shape our understanding and use of methodologies in the area of values education.

Wayne Paulson, Jack Cole, Jerry Glashagel, Mick Johnson, Bob Phipps, and John Ziegler sharpened our facilitating and training skills in values education.

Ron Rising, Dorothy Williams, and Miriam Frost gave us appreciated editorial help in writing.

Thanks go to these dear friends who provided feedback on portions of the book's content: Douglas and LaVonne Anderson, Glen and Shirley Espelien, and Clint and Violet Sprain.

Special thanks to Merton Strommen for his constant encouragement and support during the seven years we worked together at Youth Research Center, now called Search Institute. His openness to new approaches gave impetus to developing much that is in this book.

We are also grateful to three of our children — Tom, Mary Lee, and Jane Larson-Wipf, for contributing their ideas and reactions throughout the book's period of development.

Lastly, we acknowledge valuable input from workshop participants throughout the country. In our interaction with them, we tested and modified our ideas and methods. These many persons contributed to our own understanding and personal growth.

To representatives of two generations touching our lives,
   our parents,

Elvina and Elmer Linell and Judith and Petrus Larson,
who provided a caring, loving, and faithful atmosphere to
nurture faith, our values, and growth; and
   our children,
Dan, Tom, Jane, and Mary Lee,
who helped us translate our values as we journeyed as a
family through one decade into the next.

Table of Contents

Foreword

"It is all about faith!" "Nurturing the faith is child-rearing, plain and simple!" "If we want spiritually rich children, then we must have spiritually rich adults." These are phrases spoken often by one of the keynote speakers at a *Child In Our Hands* Conference sponsored by the Youth and Family Institute of Augsburg College in Minneapolis, MN. The Institute has developed a conceptual model for Christian ministries of the 21st century to pass on the faith effectively from generation to generation.

This new paradigm has a focus on the home as the primary place for nurturing faith and values and the congregation in partnership with the home. Faith is nurtured through personal, trusted relationships. The positive role of parents, grandparents, godparents, uncles, aunts, mentors, and other adult care givers is essential in the development of healthy youth, healthy families, healthy congregations, and healthy communities.

A child's faith journey is surrounded by the home. The home is surrounded by the congregation. The congregation is in the midst of a specific community. The community is within a culture. They all interact and influence the faithlife development of a child and the well-being of a family. The cross of Jesus, the Christ, reaches out to and is centered in each of these circles.

Although this book was originally written decades before the development of the conceptual model of *The Child In Our Hands*, the authors, Roland and Doris Larson, have provided an excellent resource which fits within the model in the areas of Intergenerational Enrichments Events and Christian Parenting Enrichment. Roland and Doris lived out the designs in this book long before they wrote of the designs. In the writing of this resource they are preaching what they have compassionately and passionately practiced. Faith in Christ and the values of the Christian faith are central to a healthy child, youth, and family.

In our present society there is much concern about values. A return to traditional family values is a platform for political candidates, a forum for educators, discussions and debates for philosophers, and sermons for theologians and preachers. Will the next generation have any values from which to provide leadership to communities and nations?

Dr. Roland Martinson, Senior Associate of the Youth and Family Institute of Augsburg College and Professor of Pastoral Care at Luther Seminary in St. Paul, MN has answered the question by saying, "It is impossible for a family **not** to pass on values and faith. The question really is, 'What faith and which values?'"

How Families Pass On Values and Faith

There is no laboratory in life more powerful than domestic existence. Stated faith and values are shaped, learned, celebrated, and lived out in this laboratory. Values and faith are shaped within families as follows:

- **Bonding and Attachment**

  Bonding of the parent to the child is the occasion for the birth of the conscience. This bonding has four components: emotional, physical, volitional, and spiritual.

  To attach is the fundamental step in passing on values. In the attachment is the value of self and the trust of another.

- **Atmosphere**

  A child during pregnancy is influenced by the atmosphere of a family, but even more dramatically when born. The warmth, openness, care, closeness of relationships , and valuing the unique gifts each member brings to the family, strengthens the foundations to pass on values and faith.

- **Lifestyle**

  How a family chooses to live, what they do with leisure time, how they spend their money, with whom do they spend their time, where they like to travel, how they maintain a home? — all influence the development and passing on of values and faith.

- **Roles**

  The various roles chosen by family members such as: judge/decision-maker, clown, primary provider, the sage, the healer, the savior, the historian, etc., provide models which pass on values and faith.

- **Traditions and Rituals**

  This is how a family finds ways to make memories. Routines, rituals, family traditions, celebrations are how events are brought into meaning. The telling of the stories of the traditions and rituals is as important as the events themselves.

- **Rules**

  There are written and spoken rules which a family makes, clarifies, rationalizes, and carries out expectation and responsibility. They provide the boundaries in which love is lived. There are also unwritten family rules of which a person is not aware until he or she breaks one.

- **Stated Values and Faith**

  Families have codes of arms, of values and faith. They have both bold and faint statements of faith. They develop little family sayings of stated values.

In the passing on of values and faith one should not underestimate the power of story. From the very first step of bonding and attachment God's story must be present as well as time for talking to the living God. Also from the bonding must come the parent's story and the parent's God story. There must be more than the telling of the story. There must be the family living out the story in shared service to others. What we do with the story is what children receive and understand.

In this book Roland and Doris Larson take us through these steps of passing on values and faith. The use of Scripture is very helpful in the connecting of values and faith. They acknowledge that values continually brood in, over, and around the laboratory of domestic life. It is the Holy Breath of God which gives and sustains life. The inductive process of this book evokes free and candid expressions of personal values and faith in a non threatening and receptive atmosphere.

This book provides a variety of fun designs for a family to use in the home or a congregation to use in intergenerational events, family retreats, parenting workshops, faith sharing classes and many more all to strengthen the home to teach, nurture, and pass on the faith to the next generation.

Dr. Dick Hardel

Executive Director of the Youth and Family

Institute of Augsburg College

Four Keys For Nurturing FaithLife In The Home

1. Caring Conversation

Christian values and faith are passed on to the next generation through supportive conversation. Listening and responding to the daily concerns of our children, makes it easier to have meaningful conversation regarding the love of God and is itself a way to express God's love to others.

2. Devotional Life

To pass on the Christian faith to children and youth, adults need to learn the Christian message and Biblical story as their own story. Christianity shapes the whole of one's life and, therefore, involves a lifetime of Christian study, reflection, and prayer.

3. Service

Children, youth, and adults are more likely to be influenced by those who walk the talk. The Christian talk is expressed in the Good Samaritan story. The action of the talk becomes a walk, a way of life, which communicates the care of others, and especially the care of those in need. Service projects are best done with family members and other intergenerational contact from a faith community.

4. Rituals and Traditions

Daily routines, celebrations, and other ways families choose to identify who they are and tell their family stories speak volumes about what the family values, believes, and promotes.

Values and Faith

Introduction

This book contains many practical exercises which can be used in a variety of ways — particularly with large and small groups in church-related settings or within the family. Its purpose is to help create a positive, caring, supportive environment in which individuals of all ages have an opportunity to:

- share with each other and learn from one another;
- look at what is important in their own lives;
- examine their own opinions, attitudes, beliefs, and values in a Christian context;
- discover congruencies or discrepancies between what they do and what they say they believe and value;
- take actions to make their behaviors more consistent with their beliefs and values;
- learn and practice a way to continually examine their beliefs and values;
- feel better about themselves through constructive, positive human interaction.

Too Many Choices

Recently a friend expressed thankfulness at not being a teenager in today's world. "The choices would do me in," she confided. "When I think about how many things kids have to decide nowadays, I wish I knew some way to help." Then she sighed and smiled ruefully, "But telling them doesn't do the job anymore, does it?"

Indeed it doesn't. But "telling them" didn't do the job for us either. Like the youth of today, we face many choices, too. Many of us are confused and groping for help in clarifying our priorities and values. We, too, need the opportunity to explore, to share, and to say out loud our opinions, thoughts, and ideas on important matters. We need to be listened to and to listen to others as we clarify our beliefs and values in these changing and challenging times.

We need to think about the ways we were helped in the past and decide how we will help others today.

Advice used to be one of the chief ways we tried to help other people make choices. But for the most part, the time is gone when a person can hope to achieve change in another's behavior or belief simply by outlining what ought to be done.

It's a pity, too. *Moralizing* — telling "the way it ought to be" — is such a nice, easy method for the person who assumes the role of teacher or helper or counselor. It's relatively simple for one who has lived through a given experience or time of life to tell someone younger or less experienced how to handle a new situation. Imparting the wisdom of age and experience also gives us an ego boost; it makes us feel helpful and good. But the chief drawback to moralizing is that it just doesn't work.

Moralizing is, of course, only one of the time-tested and much-venerated methods we have used to help people make choices. Another method, usually adopted by people who have tried the first one and failed, is the *laissez-faire* technique — throwing up the hands and saying, "I can't do a thing about it. Since you won't listen to me, you'll have to figure it out on your own." Even when accompanied by fervent hopes that everything will turn out right, the use of laissez-faire simply seems to make recipients suspect that people don't really care what happens to them.

Modeling — teaching by example — is a third, widely-respected method for influencing and guiding the behavior and choices of another person. In some situations, modeling seems to work. We do find people — influenced not by conscious teaching but by modeling — who imitate an admired person. Modeling has drawbacks, however. We seldom know how many people our own example affects. Moreover, few of us have the patience or the opportunity to bide our time and observe how well the modeling works. But most importantly, too many models, as well as the inconsistent behavior some of these models display, can confuse those who are trying to make decisions on the basis of what their "heroes" do.

Suggestions, guidelines, and pressures impinge on people from a host of varied sources — Mom and Dad, playmates, fellow students, teachers, church leaders, TV commercials, movie stars, popular magazines. Confusion often results from trying to determine which source is right.

Although we are concerned with passing on certain values that are important to us, down deep we know it's futile to impose them on others. But we can create an open, accepting, loving environment which encourages persons to examine various choices and find answers that make sense for their own lives.

Background For This Book

Values and Faith grew out of our experiences over the years in conducting many value-clarifying classes, seminars, workshops, and study programs for people of all ages in a wide variety of settings.

We have discovered that well-thought-out exercises, presented in an encouraging and accepting atmosphere, cause learning that leads to informed choices and changed lives. Typically, we discover enthusiasm, eagerness, and seriousness of purpose breaking out in these sessions. In one group, a 92-year-old told us, with a twinkle in her eye, "Learning in the church should always be fun like this." Likewise, kindergarteners have enthusiastically entered into similar exercises, conducted at their level of understanding.

One concern has frequently surfaced in these groups: Where can a person obtain a collection of value-clarifying exercises specifically designed for use in a Christian context? Values and Faith is our attempt to provide an answer to that question.

Viewpoint

We, the authors, assume throughout this book that God is the absolute, the beginning point of ourselves and of our world. God loves us and acts to become known to us through the Bible, the Church, the life of Christ, and the activity of the Holy Spirit among us — revealing God's will to us through what we read, what we learn from other people, and what we experience every day.

We hope the values exercises described in *Values and Faith* will help raise people's awareness of God's presence in their lives and thus help them become more conscious of the wealth of resources available for making decisions about life. This is a book to help stretch our minds and to keep us growing. We are aware, not only of the resources outside ourselves, but of the resources within. As Jesus said, "The Kingdom of God is within you."

Jesus used ways similar to some of these values exercises to help people clarify choices. He frequently laid out important questions — in what must have been, at times, a disturbing and challenging way — to make people think through the implications of what they were doing. "For what does it profit a man, to gain the whole world, and forfeit his life? For what can a man give in return for his life?" (Luke 9:25)

Jesus also told stories and asked people what they learned from them. After telling the parable of the two sons whose father sent them to a vineyard, Jesus asked, "Which of the two did the will of his father?" (Matthew 21:31) This question must have caused some thought in His day, as it does in ours. Or, following the parable of the Good Samaritan, "Which of these three, do you think, proved neighbor to the man who fell among the robbers?" (Luke 10:36)

Effective education does not give people answers; rather, it draws their own answers from them. Answers given are easily forgotten; answers discovered from within are remembered. *Values and Faith* raises questions, compelling individuals to discover answers from within themselves.

Some of what we do in this book will be recognized by those who know the values-clarification work done by Raths, Harmin, Kirschenbaum and Simon, as they developed it. They have greatly influenced our methodology. We have used, adapted, and modified parts of their approach and have found the resulting values exercises to be excellent tools for Christian education in a variety of settings: young adult programs, intergenerational events, church schools, youth groups, Bible study groups, parent groups, retreats, camps, boards and councils, special-interest small groups, family discussions.

Use in the Family

We have found practical use for these exercises with families. In our own home, we used some exercises at the mealtime table, around a fireplace or campfire, in the car, on a family vacation. Many parents who have used values exercises in their homes have been pleased to find new kinds of discussions, more openness in communications, and shared decision making within the family.

Enhancing the Learning Process

Our own excitement about using values exercises with the family and with church groups comes from seeing the following things happen in the learning process:

1. *The learner participates actively.* Discussion, we have always thought, is an improvement on most lectures. If we are free to talk, we are more interested. We have sometimes gone to sleep when other people are talking but never while outlining our beliefs to someone else! Many of the exercises in this book invite participants to talk out their beliefs with one another, with partners, or with small groups. To counteract passivity, participants are often active physically. Sometimes the action involves walking around, crossing the room, finding a particular location within the room. This process gets people involved — even

those who may have privately decided beforehand to sit on the sidelines. People don't fall asleep when they're involved; they're too busy doing things, and when they do things they remember them.

2. *The resources of the total group are used.* As long as there's only one teacher, the resources of a group are limited to what comes out of the thinking of that one person. All of us together can contribute more than any one of us. Getting everyone involved gives all of us a greater fund of information and feelings to draw on. It has been our experience that — far from causing everyone to think and act alike — the group experience causes people to become more individual, more of what they want to be.

3. *The leader or parent participates as a learner.* As a group leader or parent you have certain responsibilities that other participants do not have. But you are also free to participate along with the others in the activity of valuing. No matter how often we have used them, we always learn from these exercises. Something has changed about us since the last time we did them, or someone new in the group changes it for us — something happens that helps us learn.

4. *The learner changes.* People seldom leave a session quite the same as they began it. Something happens to them. They change their beliefs slightly, or they widen their concept of a particular issue, or they stumble onto new questions that they had never before asked of themselves.

5. *People learn to minister to one another.* In the process of clarifying values, participants have an opportunity to make their witness to one another and to be heard. Both are a way of giving and receiving ministry. We do not have to talk about the ministry of the laity and hope that somewhere people will minister to one another; we can help it happen right here, within the session.

6. *People learn to listen to one another.* Through sharing with others and respecting one another, people learn to appreciate each other's viewpoints. People get to know each other better as persons and begin to discover and understand one another in new ways. Sometimes they even find themselves enlightened, appreciative, instructed.

Although you may begin with the values exercises given here, you might soon begin constructing some of your own. You may find your whole teaching and learning pattern altered, opened up, freed to help more new things happen in your work, in your own family, in your life.

This book, then, comes filtered through our own thinking and experience with many different kinds of groups, all seeking answers for their lives. We hope that you and the people with whom you interact will find it helpful.

Leadership

Resources within People

As a leader using *Values and Faith,* you do not have to have all the answers, for you will not be teaching, in the usual sense of the word. Rather, you will be facilitating a process in which people grow and minister to each other through sharing their beliefs, attitudes, and experiences. We've learned that people have great resources within themselves to help one another think about fife's important matters.

Resources of the Christian Faith

These values exercises, however, do not propose "the blind leading the blind." Christians share a rich background of biblical history, a body of writings of religious thinkers. They believe that God acts in human history, especially through the life of Jesus and the ever-present activity of the Holy Spirit. In addition to making use of the person-resources in the group, we also assume that you will draw on the great resources of the Christian faith in presenting a framework within which people can test assumptions and make decisions.

How and when should these resources be brought into the discussion? Feel free to trust your own sense of what will be most appropriate for your situation and for your group.

Our main caution is to avoid imposing your own ideas on the group; rather, involve group members in a discovery process — using all available resources as guides.

Ideally, you will have received some group leadership training. (We realize, however, this is not always possible.) Familiarity with values theories, rationale, and methodology are recommended, as well, and we have provided a bibliography for this purpose.

Caring, Accepting Leadership

More important, however, we hope you will be a caring, warm, genuine, and accepting person. A good leader is a person first and an expert second. Techniques and methods are helpful, but your sensitivity, acceptance of others, and support for them are essential. Using these exercises, you will be most effective as a leader if you have these characteristics -

• You are open and willing to learn along with others.

• You want to be more accepting.

• You want to grow.

• You wish to increase your listening skills because you are really interested in what other people think and feel, even though you might disagree with them.

• You realize you might not have all the "right" answers for complex problems and issues, especially the problems and issues that others face.

Creating an Atmosphere

Creating an atmosphere is a highly important function of the leader. Without it, the exercises may become mere games. They are far too potentially meaningful to be used only as time-fillers or only for fun. Their purpose is serious, and though fun often occurs for people who use them, the fun is merely a fortunate by-product.

To create the necessary atmosphere, clearly indicate the guidelines which all will follow during the exercises. If you post them as well, participants may remember them better.

The following are guidelines for participants:

1. *Everyone has the tight to pass.* Every person is permitted *not* to give his or her answer to a question. The signal for passing is to fold the arms or to say "I pass." An answer of "pass" is just as acceptable as any other answer. If the atmosphere is properly established, very

few people pass after the first few minutes. Remind people occasionally that they have this right and may exercise it.

2. *Accept each other.* Encourage the group to accept the answer a person gives as the right one for him or her at that time. Remind people of this guideline if arguments or challenges of statements occur. We have grown up so used to arguing and challenging one another that accepting other views is foreign to us. But acceptance contributes greatly to an atmosphere of trust and openness. Children are great correctors of one another, often denying the feeling behind a statement as well as its accuracy: "Oh, you did not. You're just making that up; you don't either like strawberries better than cherries." But children enjoy the freedom of the accepting atmosphere when they find they can trust it. So do adults.

3. *Speak for yourself.* Encourage participants to say what they think and what they feel. (A nonjudgmental climate facilitates the use of this guideline.) But ask them to relate their comments to themselves rather than to speak for others. For example: say "I think . . ." rather than "Most of us . . ." or "We . . . ."

4. *Expect unfinished business.* Unfinished business occurs when you have more to say on a values issue or when you're curious about something someone else said and would like to explore the thought further. Having to stop a discussion or having to move on to another subject before everything has been said by everyone is a fact of the process. Remind the group at the beginning of every session that they will have unfinished business with other members of the group. Encourage them to complete it between exercises, at break time (if you have one), or after the session.

In the next section, there are some other important ideas which can increase the effectiveness of your leadership. You should have them firmly in your mind.

Further Suggestions for the Leader

In using this process most effectively, you *put aside the function of judge* which is often an accepted part of the teacher's role. Do not feel compelled to decide, as a judge would, whether an answer is good or bad, right or wrong. In your verbal acknowledgments try to avoid comments that imply either a negative or a positive reaction. When participants generate conflicting ideas and responses, leader acknowledgments such as "good," "you don't mean that do you?", "fine," "great," "that's right," "that's not right, is it?" indicate particular approval of one response over another. Acceptable acknowledgments that are not judgmental would be "thank you," and "O.K." To be a group facilitator who is nonjudgmental, we think it is important for you to —

present a stimulus (the exercise);

elicit responses to the stimulus;

accept those responses;

help each person clarify what he or she means by that response;

accept again.

At some point, *join the group* in giving your own answer or response to the exercise. It is a good idea, as in voting for instance, to delay your response a bit so that the group doesn't mirror your viewpoint. But do join them. You are a participant as well as a presenter, leader, facilitator. And your participation is valuable in several ways. First, your participation will encourage other individuals in the group to see themselves as participants with you in a shared venture. Second, what you value, how you vote, what you choose, will be observed and listened to. If you want to be influential — to have your preferences, values, choices known — this is an opportunity to present them, without foisting them on anyone. Finally, it is also important for the group to know that you, the leader, are not asking them to do something you're not willing to do yourself.

The Basic Exercises

Each of the next chapters in this book present several basic exercises as a means to explore chapter topics in depth. On pages 19 through 34, the basic exercises you will be using are thoroughly described. An explanation of how to present and share each of these simple exercises is also given. These exercises are -

Voting

Ranking

Continuum

Either/Or

Listening

Dilemma

Interviewing

Goal Setting

Each of the remaining chapters explores specific topics using examples of the exercises.

You may choose to present a seminar or workshop around a particular theme from a chapter; for example, you might develop a seminar for couples based on the exercises presented in "Valuing My Family." We have noted the specific exercises which deal with marriage, divorce, roles of husbands and wives, etc., and you can choose a combination of them for your seminar.

Using Values Exercises. in the Family

At a leisurely evening meal a news item triggered a thought: "How awful to be blind!" Using the values exercise of Ranking, we asked our children to rank in 1, 2, 3-order this question:

Which condition would you least prefer?

____ blindness

____ deafness

____ paralysis

We all voiced our rankings without discussion or judgment. Then each of us talked about our ranking, explaining the reason for that particular order of choice. In the process, we learned something new about one of our daughters. She least preferred deafness. For her, deafness would be most difficult to live with because she would miss hearing beautiful music. We could tell from the way she responded that her love of music was deep — deeper than we realized. Through this simple values exercise we gained new insight into her feelings, and she was able to verbalize those feelings to us.

Sometimes these values exercises can be helpful in complex decision making within the family. Recently, tragedy struck the family of one of our friends. The youngest of three children, a seven-year-old, was hit by a car and killed on her way home from school. That evening the parents and the two children began making plans for the funeral. In this time of sudden grief, a question arose which the family needed to deal with immediately: How shall we take care of the body? Their spontaneous inclination for this family decision was to explore the options through a values Ranking:

____ We prefer a conventional burial.

____ We prefer to donate her body for organ transplants.

____ We prefer to cremate her body.

After individual ranking and discussion, a family decision was reached — to offer the child's body for organ transplants. The wisdom of their decision was confirmed when letters arrived, thanking them for eyesight restored to others. After transplants, the body was donated to medical science for training of pediatric physicians.

Careful Family Use

You might find Ranking, Voting, and the Either/Or exercises (see pages 30-35) the easiest to use within the family. It is important to remember that these exercises are not games. They should be used responsibly with openness, acceptance, sharing, listening, and facilitating. This is not easy. We have seen meaningful discussions suddenly become threatening to the parent's or authority figure's own personal beliefs and values. Then the temptation to impose one's own beliefs is strong, and the sharing session can become simply an advice-giving lecture. At that moment of disagreement, the challenge is to listen to the other people and try to feel accepting toward them. Acceptance does not mean that you will always agree with them. As parents, you will express your own ideas along with everyone else. Your children will want and need to know where you stand. Acceptance means rather that family members are willing to help each other express themselves; that together families can build a climate in which each person's ideas, thoughts, and feelings are respected; that they can leam to share in a spirit of mutual trust and understanding. Within this kind of climate, family members can clarify their own personal values and help each other to build strong family relationships.

Eight Basic Exercises

Eight basic exercises are used in *Values and Faith*. Nearly all of the following types will be found in each of the book's sections.

The insignia shown below will be used to help you quickly locate and identify each of the eight basic exercises throughout the book.

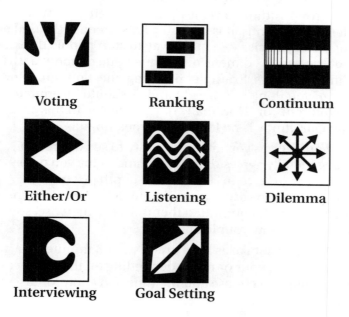

Voting	**Ranking**	**Continuum**
Either/Or	**Listening**	**Dilemma**
Interviewing	**Goal Setting**	

A description of the purpose and procedural steps for each of these eight exercises is provided in this chapter. Be familiar with these steps before using the exercises. Have them at your fingertips and refer to them frequently.

Each section of the book also includes a variety of additional exercises, often one of a kind. Instructions are included with each of these miscellaneous exercises.

Voting

Definition and Purpose:

The *Voting* exercise consists of a series of statements or questions to which participants respond by agreeing or disagreeing with each statement or question.

Voting gives each participant a chance, without talking, to take a stand and to note the responses of the rest of the group. Although values Voting is useful in a wide variety of situations, it is probably most frequently used as an opening exercise — a quick way to start people thinking about the various dimensions of one issue or about a variety of different issues. Examples of Voting questions are "How many of you think the size of families should be limited to two children?" or "How many of you agree with this statement: Our liturgy is no longer very meaningful?"

Voting gives you an opportunity to see where the group generally agrees or disagrees and helps you determine where to "zero in" for more in-depth discussion. Participate in the voting yourself, but delay your response until others have committed themselves. Otherwise, some will tend to follow your lead.

Voting can take as little time as 2 or 3 minutes. Or it may require an hour or more, depending on the number of voting items you choose and the time you allow for discussion.

Procedure:

1. Before you begin the exercise, give these instructions: "I will be asking questions or reading statements to which I'd like your response. If you agree, raise your hand high. Wave it if you agree strongly. If you disagree, make a fist and put your thumb down. Shake it if you disagree strongly. If you wish, you may pass by folding your arms across your chest. Do this if you have no opinion on the question, or if you don't want to answer the question."

2. Give participants a chance to try out the hand positions by asking one or two questions. Each time start with "How many of you...?" or "How many of you agree with the following statement?" Repeat each question or statement so that everyone has a chance to hear it.

3. Judge how much, if any, discussion you will allow. Voting moves quickly, but certain issues need to be discussed in depth. You may want to set aside time for discussion or allow brief discussion on the spot.

At any time during or after the exercise you may wish to draw from our Christian heritage resources that pertain to the topic. Be sure to elicit contributions from group members as well.

Ranking

Definition and Purpose:
The *Ranking* exercise presents three or more possible choices for participants to rearrange in their order of preference or priority (for example, from best to worst, or from most important to least important).

Ranking helps participants consider different options and make their own personal choices. Through the process of ranking or prioritizing, persons examine their thoughts, attitudes, feelings, beliefs, and behaviors. Ranking gives participants practice in choosing among alternatives and provides opportunities to explain and defend their choices, while being exposed to the thinking and choices of others.

Several Rankings can be done in 10-15 minutes. More time must be allotted if small- or large-group discussions are planned following the exercise.

Here is an example of a Ranking exercise:

What time of the year do you enjoy most with your family?

____ Easter

____ Thanksgiving

____ Christmas

Procedure:

1. Read a question or statement with three or more different response items, writing them on newsprint or on a chalkboard if possible.

2. Sometimes all items are appealing and meaningful. Sometimes none of them is. In either case, ask people to rank all the items in order of importance or preference to them (1 most important; 2 = next most important, etc.).

3. Invite volunteers to share their rankings and their reasons. After accepting seven or eight responses, you may wish to give your own ranking, with reasons why.

Sharing might also take place in small groups, with each group including persons who made different rank orders. Allow time for discussion.

Again, bring resources from our Christian heritage to the discussion.

Continuum

Definition and Purpose:
The *Continuum* exercise presents two opposite choices or viewpoints. Respondents select that place on the continuum — between the choices — which most closely represents their personal views.

A wide array of response is possible on many value issues. The Continuum exercise opens the possibility for many gradations of choice between two extremes. Participants examine their own opinions and beliefs and take stands where they feel most comfortable between the extremes. In addition, they become aware of the range of views that exist in the thinking of a seemingly homogeneous group of people. Discussing one's point of view with another person often brings the issue into clearer focus and helps participants improve their ability to hear and understand one another.

A Continuum exercise can sometimes be done quickly in 5 or 10 minutes. However, more time is often needed, depending upon the amount and intensity of discussion which follows.

Here is an example of a Continuum exercise:

What should be the main emphasis in church life?

|————————————————————————————————|

Worship Services   Social Action

Procedure:

1. Ask a question which raises an issue. Then describe two disparate responses to that issue.

2. Designate an imaginary line across the room, asking participants to respond to the issue by placing themselves at a point on the line representing their own personal view. (Afterward, you may wish to take your own position on the continuum.)

3. Encourage participants to share reasons for their choices with one or two people nearby.

4. After a few minutes, elicit from several people (particularly those at the extremes) their reasons for standing where they are. Focus on respondents, listening and accepting their statements.

5. General discussion may then follow. Or discussion might be continued in small groups.

If you decide on small-group discussion, number off the total group (1, 2, 3, 4; 1, 2, 3, 4, etc.) from one end of the continuum to the other. Have all one's meet together, two's together, etc.

Later, come together and share discoveries, learnings, and observations. Questions to consider: 1) As a result of the sharing, did anyone get an insight that encouraged you to change your position? 2) What did you learn from this experience?

If Continuum exercises are used in sequence, have people come to the middle of the room each time before announcing the next issue and describing the two extreme positions.

At some point, you may introduce data and material from Christian resources, asking, for example, "What does God's Word say about this issue? Let's search it out together."

Either/Or

Definition and Purpose:
The *Either/Or* exercise is a forced choice between tw options. Respondents select the option with which they most closely identify.

Often a choice boils down to one of two alternatives. Sometimes both choices are appealing; sometimes neither one is. Nevertheless, people are often forced to choose one of two options. In this exercise, participants are asked to examine choices and are exposed to the choices and thoughts of others.

Here is an example of an Either/Or choice:
Which are you most like?

leader / follower

Either/Or is sometimes set up as a metaphorical exercise. For example, you might ask participants, "Which are you more like, a hardwood floor or wall-to-wall carpeting?" Participants exercise their imaginations and intuitions to relate themselves to these items, considering the implications of each choice: Am I plain or fancy? Do I prefer things simple or luxurious? Am I old-fashioned or modern?

Time required for the Either/Or exercise is variable. Plan for a minimum of 10 minutes. If multiple Either/Or exercises are used, you may wish to shift to another type of exercise after 20-25 minutes.

Procedure:

1. Clear the room so that people can move about easily.

2. Ask a question with two alternatives. Repeat it.

3. Point to the opposite sides of the room and ask those identifying with the first alternative to go to one side and those identifying with the second alternative to the other.

4. Have each participant find a partner on the same side and share reasons for their choices with each other. (Or, people can find partners at the opposite side and share.) In general, limit discussion on an item to about 2 or 3 minutes.

5. Before the next Either/Or choice, call the group to the middle of the room, so that an active choice has to be made each time.

Listening

Definition and Purpose:

The *Listening* exercise consists of a stimulus statement or paragraph to which each person in a group of three responds individually while the others listen to him or her. The individual responder is called the *focus person.*

Small groups typically carry on discussions which are dominated by a few people, while other members seldom are encouraged or have a chance to express their ideas. The Listening exercise gives all group members equal time to express their personal views and reactions to an issue. When closely followed, this exercise provides an opportunity for each person to be listened to and to be a listener. Each Listening exercise requires 20 minutes or more to complete.

Controversial statements provide the content to which participants respond. For example, a statement might be read which suggests a controversial way in which a worship service should be conducted.

Procedure:

Prior to beginning the exercise:

1. Select a content area for discussion and choose an appropriate Listening statement.

2. Divide the total group into smaller groups of three.

3. Have groups sit together while you give the instructions.

4. Announce that a provocative statement will soon be made and that each person will have an opportunity to respond to the statement, receiving the full attention of the other two group members.

5. Give the following guidelines for the Listening exercise (post these guidelines, stressing their importance to successful completion of the exercise):

Focusing   Give these instructions:

Taking turns, each person will be on focus for 5 minutes. During this period the focus person will respond to the Listening statement — commenting on it, agreeing or disagreeing with portions of it, adding new thoughts. Other group members should not let the attention shift from the focus person. While focusing on another's comments, hold your own thoughts or reactions until it is your turn to be on focus.

Drawing Out   Give these instructions:

Listen as intently as you can. You may not agree with what the focus person says, but try not to indicate this in any way, for the time being. Instead, try to understand his or her attitudes, beliefs, and feelings. Ask questions to help clarify the focus person's comments and feelings, but do not allow attention to shift from the focus person to yourself.

Acceptance   Give these instructions:

Try to feel accepting, even when you don't agree with what the focus person is saying. You can demonstrate your acceptance by listening, smiling, and nodding.

Keep eye contact; be warm and supportive. And then listen some more!

Begin the exercise:

1. Ask each group to designate the first focus person.

2. Read the selected Listening statement and ask the focus person in each group to begin talking.

3. When 5 minutes are up, ask groups to stop wherever they are and move clockwise to the next focus person. (Repeat until each has had a turn.)

4. By this point, many individual reactions typically have been generated within the small groups. They may want to simply talk and share for a few minutes. Allow for normal small-group conversation so that some feeling of closure on the subject matter is reached.

5. Reassemble the total group and share learnings, observations. Ask, "Does the Word of God speak to this issue? What does it say?" Then talk about it: in the total group, or in small groups again.

 # Dilemma

Definition and Purpose:
A values *Dilemma is* a story that presents a dilemma but stops short of the solution. Participants try to solve the dilemma.

Values Dilemmas give participants practice in generating alternative solutions and considering the possible consequences of each. Based on the data generated, they choose a "best" solution to the problem.

The time required for a dilemma is usually 20-30 minutes, sometimes more.

Here is an example of a Dilemma: You are a high school junior. A person representing a social agency in your neighborhood speaks at your church. His message is interesting, but you feel he unjustly criticizes the young people in your community's churches for their "lack of concern for other youth." You think he is not in touch with what the youth in the churches are attempting to do. By the time he finishes, you are furious. As you leave the church, you notice that the speaker is greeting people at the door. You will have to pass by him on your way out. STOP

What could you do right now? What might happen?

Procedure:

1. Have participants form small discussion groups of 3-4 and sit together. Pass out paper to each group; then read the Dilemma story.

2. Give the following steps, asking that they be followed carefully:

Step one: Brainstorm. Give these instructions to the group:

Each small group brainstorm together all possible alternative responses to the dilemma-situation and list them on your paper. List the possibilities quickly *without discussing or judging,* at this point, whether or not they will work. See how many you can list in 4 minutes.

Step two: Consider consequences of each alternative.

After 5 minutes, continue with these instructions: Go over your list, one item at a time. As you look at each alternative, discuss what possible consequences it might have. jot them down. (Move from group to group to monitor the progress. Many groups are ready to move from Step two after 6-8 minutes.)

Step three: Make a decision. Give these instructions:

Each person make an individual decision. Consider also the Christian perspective. What would you personally do? Choose one response.

Prior to beginning Step four, challenge people to really try to hear one another. Allow ample time for listening and understanding.

Step four: Share individual responses. Give these instructions:

In your small groups, take turns explaining why you made your particular decision.

Step five: Reflect on choices. Give these instructions:

In your groups, reflect on these questions: Did Christianity have anything to do with the choice you made? What? Do the Scriptures provide any guidelines for this situation?

3. Reassemble the entire group.

4. Ask for volunteers to tell the total group what their decision was. Then ask for any other key ideas that emerged in the small groups.

Some small groups may wish to role play their best solution and possibly reenact their situation for the entire group. Why not give an invitation to do so?

 # Interviewing

Definition and Purpose:
The values Interview consists of questions asked by the leader of a volunteer from the group.

Interviewing gives that volunteer an opportunity to share some information with the total group about self, personal thoughts, feelings, attitudes, and values. The Interview allows the group to learn from the life of another in a short time. It is an excellent way to help people in ongoing groups and classes to get acquainted and understand one another.

Time required for a public Interview is often 15-20 minutes. An additional 20 minutes must be allotted for a paired Interview.

An Interview might be used, for example, with a Confirmation class. A class member is interviewed in order for the group to learn about that person's life, experiences, beliefs, and values. (You can also interview someone from outside the group. In this case, perhaps, a pastor, youth worker, or someone recently confirmed.)

Procedure:

Interviewing before a group:

1. Explain that you would like to conduct an interview with someone from the group.

2. Select the interviewee or ask for a volunteer. While people are thinking (and perhaps hesitating), announce these simple ground rules for the interview:

   - The person to be interviewed answers honestly and openly.

   - The interviewee has the right to pass on any question.

   - The interviewee controls the interview. At any point he or she can terminate the interview by stating, "Thanks for the interview." The interviewer (you) can bring it to a close in the same manner.

   - When the interview is completed, the person interviewed will have the privilege of asking the interviewer any question he or she was asked.

3. In selecting a volunteer, you can interview the first person who responds, or you can wait until three or four have volunteered and then choose one. Quickly review the ground rules, or ask the interviewee to restate them in his or her own words.

4. Proceed with the interview, allowing about 10-15 minutes for completion. It is important to keep track of time and not carry the interview on too long, especially with children.

5. Begin with questions which elicit basic information. For example:

   - What is your full name?

   - Where did you grow up as a child?

   - Do you have brothers and sisters?

   - Where did you attend school?

   - What hobbies do you have now?

6. Use your own style to listen, to reflect thoughts and feelings, to paraphrase, and to ask more questions, but add no input of your own. (Focus on the person being interviewed; do not discuss the person's responses.) As you begin to hear attitudes, beliefs, values, you may go into some depth as seems appropriate — sometimes following the interviewee's train of thought, sometimes changing to a desired topic with a direct question again.

7. If the group has been dealing with a certain topic, the interviewee can be asked some questions or opinions about it. Here is also a chance to find out about the person's background, experience, and thoughts about the church. You might want to ask questions like these:

   • Did you attend church as a child? Where?

   • Did you attend church school or Sunday school?

   • Was there a particular class or teacher you liked best?

   • Have you been involved in any church activities or groups during the last five years?

   • What is your most meaningful church involvement now?

   • Was there any one person in your life who had an influence on what you believe now? Do you care to share anything about it?

8. At the end, give the interviewee the option to question the interviewer.

Interviewing in pairs:

A follow-up to the exercise described above is to involve everyone in an interview, at the same time, in pairs.

1. Instruct the participants to find a partner — someone in the group they don't know very well.

2. Explain that in each pair, one person is the interviewer, the other the interviewee.

3. After 6-8 minutes, call time. Have pairs switch roles, and begin a final interview.

4. Before the pairs come back to the total group, provide time for them to talk for a minute or two about their experience together, how it felt to interview and to be interviewed.

Interviews are most effective when the interviewer does not use a predetermined list of questions. If you have some general issues in mind, yet are flexible and a good listener, your interview will be comfortable and informative.

Goal Setting

Definition and Purpose:
Value learning is incomplete unless values are linked to one's commitments and behavior. Throughout this book, therefore, Goal Setting is used intennittently, often at the end of a miscellaneous exercise.

Goal Setting helps translate discussed ideas into planned action. It helps individuals to act on a decision. The individual tells others in the group of his or her goal and makes a comn-dtment to accomplish it. Thus, Goal Setting is a way of getting things done, changing something, helping a person become more the person he or she wants to be.

Sometimes Goal Setting is done as a one-time-only activity. But in groups that meet weekly (or on some other regular basis) it may be a part of each session. Setting goals is most often a closing activity and usually can be done in small groups in about 10 minutes.

Here are examples of goals which persons might set:

- To complete a specific project for school.
- To write a long overdue letter to a friend.
- To confront a person about a difficult matter.

Procedure:

1. Give this goal-setting sequence:
   - Select a goal you want to attain.
   - Carry out your plan.
   - From achieving your goal, you will feel satisfaction.
   - Set another goal, carry it out, and continue to experience more feelings of satisfaction and achievement.

2. Post these eight guidelines for goal setting and review them with the group. A goal should be —

   conceivable: can be put into words;

   believable: is appropriate to your own set of values;

   achievable: can be accomplished;

   controllable: does not depend on another person for its attainment;

   measurable: is countable, observable;

   desirable: is something you really want to achieve;

   definite: there are no alternatives — you *will* reach it — not just try to;

   beneficial: has a positive effect on a person and/or society.

   Stress the importance of following the guidelines, encouraging participants to make sure that their goals fit each. This will greatly improve the chance for successful attainment of goals. You can demonstrate how this works by setting a personal goal, stating it to the group, and showing how it fits each of the guidelines.

3. Sometimes participants can set goals quietly and alone. At other times they may want to work in small groups where they can use each other as resources — discussing their ideas, formulating their goals, and finally stating the goals (word for word) to one another.

4. It is important for individuals to report the actual attainment of a goal. With ongoing groups, individuals can report to the group at the opening of the next session. If no additional session is planned, encourage participants to arrange a time by which they will check in with a specific person in their group — perhaps by telephone, or however they wish.

5. If you hold another session for the same group, provide time at the beginning for reporting on goals. You might start by saying, "My goal was ... and here's what happened Encourage others to summarize their goals and tell what happened.

Miscellaneous Exercises

At the end of each chapter, exercises appear which are one-of-a-kind. These Miscellaneous Exercises are designed to help participants further examine what they believe and value. Directions and procedures accompany each.

Three Levels of Learning

In learning we typically deal with three levels:

- Facts
- Concepts
- Values

Learning begins at the facts level. We need factual information in order to understand concepts and formulate our own values. Biblical passages contain rich material at each level. Obviously, a great amount of value-laden content is provided.

Each section of this book includes an exercise which focuses on each of the three levels. All or part of this insignia is used in those exercises.

The insignia is a reminder of the three levels. In teaching-learning activities, we think it is important to spend considerable time at the values level.

Write Your Own Exercises

You may want to write your own exercises when dealing with content areas not covered in this book. The following forms provide an outline for creating new exercises to fit specific issues or subject matter content. Winston Press, Inc. gives permission to reproduce the forms for group and family use.

Consider and complete the following items on each form:

- the setting for your group
- the group or activity you will be working with
- the age, sex, and other relevant characteristics of participants
- the value issue, goal, or objective to be considered
- methods for sharing
- helpful resources you can draw from

The outline helps develop a specific exercise to be used with a specific group of people dealing with a specific value issue in a specific way.

Prior to the group session, take time to carefully define the value issue, goal, or objective to be considered. The questions and exercises you develop should be ones that capture a group's interest and stimulate participants to think. Try out the question or exercise on one or two others in advance.

Sharing is an important part of learning; it gives participants a chance to express what they think and feel and to hear others express themselves. Using different sharing modes (pairs, small groups, large group) helps maintain interest.

Voting
Setting:
Group/activity:
Participant characteristics:

Value issue, goal, or objective:

"How many of you _____ ?"

"How many of you _____ ?"

"How many of you _____ ?"

"How many of you _____ ?"

"How many of you _____ ?"

"How many of you _____ ?"

"How many of you _____ ?"

"How many of you _____ ?"

"How many of you _____ ?"

Sharing methods:

_____ total group

_____ small groups

_____ pairs

_____ other

Resources:

Permission is given to reproduce this page for group and family use.

Ranking
Setting:
Group/activity:
Participant characteristics:
Value issue, goal, or objective:

Question " _____ ?"

(choices to be ranked)

Question " _____ ?"

(choices to be ranked)

Question " _____ ?"

(choices to be ranked)

Sharing:

_____ total group

_____ small groups who disagree

_____ small groups who agree

_____ pairs

_____ other

Resources:

Continuum

Setting:

Group/activity:

Participant characteristics:

Value issue, goal, or objective:

Question " _____ ?"
    (describe one   describe other
      extreme)   extreme)

Question " _____ ?"
    (describe one   (describe other
      extreme)   extreme)

Question " _____ ?"
    (describe one   (describe other
      extreme)   extreme)

Sharing:

_____ turn to person near you and share

_____ total group

_____ number off to form small groups of persons representing different positions

_____ other

Resources:

Permission is given to reproduce this page for group and family use.

Either/Or

Setting:

Group/activity:

Participant characteristics:

Value issue, goal, or objective:

Which do you identify more with?

_____ or _____

_____ or _____

_____ or _____

_____ or _____

_____ or _____

_____ or _____

Sharing:

_____ total group

_____ pairs who made same choice

_____ pairs who made opposite choice

_____ other

Resources:

Listening
Setting:
Group/activity:
Participant characteristics:
Value issue, goal, or objective:

Listening Statement:

Sharing:

_____ groups of 3

_____ groups of 4

_____ other

Resources:

Permission is given to reproduce this page for group and family use.

Interviewing

Setting:
Group/activity:
Participant characteristics:
Value issue, goal, or objective:

Factual or informational questions:

Deeper questions:

Sharing:

_____ interviewing in total groups

_____ interviewing in pairs

Resources:

Permission is given to reproduce this page for group and family use.

Dilemma

Setting:
Group/activity:
Participant characteristics:
Value issue, goal, or objective:

Story Outline:

Background information

Situation

Key question

Sharing:

What could you do at this point? (Options)

What would happen if you did each one? (Consequences)

What would you personally do? (Choosing, acting)

Why?

Resources:

Valuing My Faith

Values and Faith centers around the Christian faith. Faith provides the context in which persons examine their opinions, attitudes, and beliefs.

The exercises in this section are designed to help participants clarify their own personal faith and its importance in their lives. Further, the intent of these exercises is to give persons an opportunity to:

- Develop a deeper appreciation of their faith.
- Think about faith as a source of their personal values.
- Think about how their faith is related to their actions.
- Think about how their faith provides a framework for living out their lives.
- Seek to discover who Christ is to them.
- Explore areas of uncertainty and struggle in their faith life.
- Become aware of ways to share their faith and to set personal goals to accomplish this.

Before using this chapter, please review the chapter on leadership.

 ## Voting

Instructions: Pages 30-31 give purpose and procedure for the Voting exercise.

Participants vote in the following manner:

Agree?	(Raise hand.)
Strongly agree?	(Wave hand.)
Disagree?	(Thumb down.)
Strongly disagree?	(Shake thumb.)
Pass?	(Fold arms across chest.)

General Voting Questions on Faith

How many of you:

- think that faith in God "just happens?"
- find that your ideas about God have changed a lot since grade school?
- are at a loss for words when someone challenges your beliefs?
- sometimes have doubts about your faith?
- believe that God makes himself best known through Jesus?
- think that a Christian needs other people in order to live fully?
- think that every Christian should be able to identify a conversion experience in his or her life?
- think most people find it difficult to share their faith?
- think that Jesus continues to live in people through the presence of the Holy Spirit?
- think the Bible is relevant to every person's life?
- think it's important to participate in Communion at least once a month?
- think it's important to participate in Communion more than once a month?
- believe that prayers are always heard?
- think we can learn from other religious faiths?
- think that people have trouble accepting salvation as a free gift?
- view death as a beginning rather than an ending?

Faith and God

How many of you agree with this statement?

- God is always pursuing us.
- It is really difficult to know if there is a God.
- God supplies our needs.

- God gives us choices in our everyday life.
- Faith in God is based on a personal relationship with God.
- A person may believe in God and yet not have faith.
- A person may believe that God is good and yet not have faith.
- No one has ever seen God.
- We all need redemption.
- God gives a person direction in deciding what is right or wrong.
- God controls our every thought and act.
- A person can believe God is good, even when there is evil and suffering in the world.
- All evil and suffering in the world is a result of sin. Satan is real.
- Satan is the source of all evil.
- God intends only good for us.
- God suffers with us in times of tragedy.
- God daily rescues people from evil.
- God uses our sin to teach us of his love.
- God makes himself known through others.

Faith and Jesus
How many of you:

- think that Jesus is truly divine and truly human?
- think that Christ is the Son of God?
- wonder about Jesus' childhood?
- think that deep down, many Christians wish Jesus weren't Jewish?
- really rejoice that Jesus, as the Bible says, was a human being like us in all ways, but without sin?
- believe that Jesus is the only way to God?

- think that because Jesus was tempted he is better able to understand and help others who are tempted?
- believe that Jesus actually rose from the dead?
- feel that Christians must take the resurrection story literally?
- feel that it is important to prove things about Jesus, such as that he was an historical person, that he rose from the dead?
- think it is harder for us to believe in Jesus than it was for first-century Christians?

Faith and the Holy Spirit
How many of you:

- think of God in three ways — as Father, Son, and Holy Spirit?
- think belief in the Holy Spirit is less essential than belief in the Father and Jesus?
- believe that the Holy Spirit can give power to your life?
- are uncertain about the nature and working of the Holy Spirit?
- believe that God's Spirit is active in us?
- think that Jesus continues to live in people through the presence of the Holy Spirit?
- really don't understand the way the Holy Spirit works?
- ever wish for an empowering by the Holy Spirit like the early disciples received on the day of Pentecost?
- think the Holy Spirit comes to chosen people in the Church?
- believe you cannot understand or believe in Jesus except with the help of the Holy Spirit?
- think of the Holy Spirit as a counselor?
- believe that the gifts you have are the work of the Holy Spirit?

- believe that the Holy Spirit gives different gifts to people?

- believe that one needs to experience a definite "baptism by the Spirit" in order to know the Spirit?

- think the Holy Spirit is the one who makes God's Word clear to you?

- think the Holy Spirit gives people power to live for God and others?

- believe the Church is held together by the power of the Holy Spirit?

- believe that the Spirit can work in people's lives even when they are not open to it or aware of it?

Faith and the Bible

How many of you agree with this statement?

- The Bible is the Word of God.

- What a person gets out of the Bible depends on what that person brings to the Bible.

- Each person is free to interpret the Bible in his or her own way.

- Some people twist Scripture to say what they want it to say.

- The Bible is relevant to every person's life.

- The Bible provides as much insight into our problems and needs today as it provided people throughout the ages.

- Sometimes it's hard to know what the Bible originally said because of translation changes.

- The Bible contains no errors.

- The Bible is a revelation of God.

- The Bible teaches much about human nature.

- The Bible is not a science book.

- The Bible is a personal revelation, something between God and an individual.

- An important way to learn what the Bible has to say is through studying and discussing it with others.
- The Bible reveals new truths and meanings for us as we change and grow.

Baptism and Communion
How many of you:

- usually listen to a sermon as if God himself were speaking to you?
- think most people overlook the joy of the Lord's Supper?
- think that participating in the Lord's Supper makes a person more certain of God's love and forgiveness?
- feel that the Lord's Supper is a very personal experience?
- find that the promise of forgiveness in both Baptism and the Lord's Supper is a reason for rejoicing?
- view Baptism as a command of Christ?
- think a person must be baptized to be saved?
- believe God adopts a person into his family through Baptism?
- find Baptism a helpful reminder of who you are?
- think prayer is an important preparation for Communion?
- think it's important to participate in Communion as often as possible?

Life and Death
How many of you:

- think that the way you view death is related to the way you view life?
- think that death is a result of evil in the world?
- think that eternal life as Jesus promised it begins here and now?

- think it is possible to fear life more than death?
- believe in life after death?
- find God's Word a source of strength in thinking about death?
- think of your own death more as an enemy than as a friend?
- view death as a beginning rather than an ending?
- sometimes wonder just what the Creed means by "the resurrection of the body?"
- think there is a difference in the way Christians and non-Christians face death?
- think that some Christians fear death because they fear eternal punishment?

Grace

How many of you:

- think grace might mean God loving us with no strings attached?
- think that personal salvation depends solely on God?
- think most people strive to worship "properly" and live "correctly" in order to earn God's favor?
- have experienced a special instance of grace in your own life?
- find it difficult to believe God loves you even when you are at your worst?
- think that God's love for us depends on the good things we do?
- think that God's love for us depends on our belief in him?
- think that God's love for us depends on our feelings toward him?
- think that God's love for us depends on whether we refuse or accept that love?
- find the concept of grace difficult to understand?

- How many of you agree with this statement?
- God sees us as sinners whom he loves.
- God's acceptance of us depends on how much we know about the Bible.
- God is less accepting of people who use drugs or alcohol than those who don't.
- God's acceptance of us depends on how we treat our neighbor.
- All people are given God's grace; they only need to accept it.

Faith and Doubt
How many of you:

- think that faith is a gift from God?
- think that you can prove your faith by attending church regularly?
- think that we can't trust God unless we fully understand him?
- think that faith is a greater risk than downhill skiing?
- think that having a religious faith is important?
- see your faith as your highest value?
- are bothered when other people express doubts about God?
- are bothered when you have doubts about God?
- think we should be ashamed to have doubts about our religious beliefs?
- think that faith needs to be tested to be real? think that doubts often lead to real certainty about our faith?
- think that to be of help to a person who doubts, you must have experienced doubt yourself?

- think that faith is something you have to work at constantly?
- think that religion has become too academic and complicated?
- think that God never intended that religion be complicated?
- think that churches would be better off if people did not choose their religion until they were capable of making a mature choice?
- think that most people need proof of something before they will believe it?

Change through Conversion
How many of you agree with this statement?

- Conversion happens at a certain time and place.
- Conversion happens every day.
- Human nature changes at the time of conversion.
- Anger disappears at the time of conversion.
- A person can be completely changed after conversion.
- A person should be able to state definitely whether he or she is saved.
- After conversion, a person never reverts to the old self.
- Conversion is a private matter between a person and God.
- Other people are often instrumental in the conversion experience of individuals.
- If a family member or a friend is struggling with his or her life and faith, you should help them toward a conversion experience.
- Conversion happens when God breaks into a person's life.
- A person's own efforts and attitudes are important in bringing about a conversion experience.

Personal Beliefs

How many of you:

- think that belief in God is necessary for a meaningful life? have difficulty putting into words what you believe about God?

- are not sure what you really believe?

- don't think much about why you believe as you do?

- have the same basic religious beliefs as your parents?

- have beliefs that are quite different from those of your parents?

- try to pass on your beliefs to your friends or family members?

- think that one's personal faith should lead to more relationships that are supportive and caring?

- think that Christian life is meaningful only if one holds certain beliefs?

- think that any relationship to God based only on feeling is very flimsy?

Sharing Beliefs

How many of you:

- think it is impossible to persuade someone to become a Christian? think that faith is more corporate than private?

- think that if we really know what we believe, we will share that belief?

- think most Christians do not share their faith easily because they are embarrassed to talk about it with others?

- think most Christians do not share their faith easily because it is a private matter?

- think that Christians often set poor examples for non-Christians?

- have ever told another person what your faith means to you?

- think that Christians ought to respect what other people believe, without trying to alter those beliefs?
- would like to tell a friend about your faith, but don't know where to begin?
- had an opportunity to share your personal faith with someone but did not make use of it?
- shared your personal faith with someone, and it made a real difference in his or her life?
- think that preaching the Gospel is almost useless to people struggling for physical survival?
- think the best way to transmit your faith to others is to tell what it means to you?
- think the best way to transmit your faith to others is simply to live it?

Prayer
How many of you:

- often pray silently in public places?
- believe that public prayer is hypocritical?
- pray silently at work or in school?
- pray with your family?
- wish your family had prayed more when you were younger?
- would rather pray alone than in a group?
- have a set time and place for prayer each day?
- feel that praying is not necessary?
- wish you knew more about praying?
- like to pray in unison at church worship?
- feel closer to God when you pray?
- are not sure God hears when you pray?
- know that God hears your prayers?
- have experienced answers to prayer?
- think that prayer is like magic?

- prefer to pray the written prayers of others?
- usually create you own prayers?
- often use hymns as prayers?
- pray for others who are ill?
- pray mostly for your own needs?
- pray every day?
- believe that God hears prayerful requests but does not always grant them?
- think that it isn't possible for God to hear all people's prayers at the same time?
- think God often answers prayer in more than one way? pray even when you feel doubt and disbelief?
- wonder why we need to pray at all when God is all-knowing and all-wise?
- think that answers to prayer are possible but improbable?
- think God answers prayer in proportion to your faith?
- are comfortable praying? find prayer difficult?
- find it difficult to pray in public?
- are embarrassed to bow your head in public before you eat?

Christian Life
How many of you agree with this statement?

- If God is in your life, you are never a "nobody."
- The Christian faith helps you decide what's important in life.
- Personal ambition can keep you from finding faith in God.
- Personal ambition can keep you from living out faith in God.

- Christians should be able to bear more sorrows and burdens than non-Christians.
- God can use our personal tragedies to build better disciples.
- All Christians have a cross to bear.
- The Apostles' Creed should begin with the words "we believe" rather than "I believe."
- An important mission of the Church is to help liberate poor and oppressed people and to heal human misery.

How many of you:

- wonder what being a Christian really means?
- think that a Christian should not get angry?
- think Christians should always "turn the other cheek?"
- think that people should be free to dress as they wish for church?
- think that you can't be a Christian without other people?
- think that a person does not have to be an active church member to be a Christian?
- think that the local church is the main source of fellowship, support, and strength for a Christian?
- have questions about your relationship to God?
- wish you had a closer relationship to Christ?
- feel a closer relationship to God because of Christ?
- feel a closer relationship to God through other people?
- think that change is part of God's order, and nothing is absolute except God's love for us?
- think that to love God you must also love your fellow human beings?

Other Religions

How many of you agree with this statement?

- We do not learn from other faiths because we generally ignore them or actively reject them.

- Good people of non-Christian faiths are often more virtuous than Christians.

- Persons of the Christian faith generally listen carefully to the ideas of persons of other faiths. We can learn much from other groups and other cultures, but people in our church seldom take the opportunity to do so.

- Most Christians would feel uncomfortable having a Buddhist in their home. Doctrine divides, and that is why different denominations have trouble working closely together.

- The ecumenical movement can be destructive if it is carried too far.

- Non-Christians will not have eternal life with God.

- It doesn't matter so much what you believe as long as you believe in some kind of God. Different faiths are just different means to the same end. Christians should not try to convert those who believe differently.

- If all religions are seen as equally valid, the real meaning of the Christian faith is diminished.

- First-century traditions are not important to Christians today.

- Christians need to continually examine and reexamine their faith in the light of other world views.

- Both ancient and modern ideas are needed to fully understand and strengthen one's Christian faith.

- Modern science conflicts with the Christian world view.

- Evolution and the biblical account of Creation are compatible.

- The Christian faith is an extension of the Jewish faith. Most Christians have not closely examined the relationship of the Jewish Passover to the Lord's Supper.

Ranking

Instructions: Pages 31-32 give purpose and procedure for the Ranking exercise.

Participants rank all items in order of preference or priority (1 = most important; 2 = next most important, etc.)

General Faith Rankings

Which of the following would help you most in learning the meaning of faith?

____ exploring the way the Bible defines faith

____ listening to a theologian talk on faith

____ putting yourself in Jesus' hands in a risky situation

____ listening to experiences of others who have lived in faith

Faith in Jesus is most like which of these?

____ venturing into a love relationship with someone

____ knowing your parents will help you if you ask

____ trusting the airplane to get you from Minneapolis to Los Angeles

____ knowing water will come out of the tap when you turn the spigot

Which statement is most important in relating to God?

____ Doubts are okay; God understands them.

____ Faith becomes even stronger when it is tested through doubt.

____ We should never doubt.

Our salvation depends upon:

____ God's action.

____ our own works.

____ making a decision for Christ.

____ fate — it's already decided who will be saved.

Which is most important to you?

_____ faith in the ability of education to develop human potential

_____ faith in God's work in people's lives

_____ faith that science will assure continual progress

_____ faith in the goodness of people

What is the greatest hindrance to your faith in God?

_____ your own weaknesses

_____ personal tragedy

_____ faith's conflict with science

_____ difficulty in knowing God

What steps are most important after a person has put God in command of his or her life?

_____ reading the Bible and other Christian books

_____ sharing one's faith and doubts with other Christians

_____ praying and attending church

_____ caring for others

How is the Christian faith most often passed on to others?

_____ through words

_____ through personal witness

_____ through the Holy Spirit

_____ through loving actions

Faith and God
What is the most important belief you hold about God and Creation?

_____ God created the world in six days.

_____ God created man and woman.

_____ God is continually creating.

Where do you see the most evident signs of God's presence?

____ in the faith of others

____ in the life of Jesus

____ in the Bible in the world around us

What quality comes to your mind first when you think of God?

____ loving

____ stern

____ holy

____ just

____ all-knowing

____ all-powerful

____ merciful

Faith and Jesus

Which of these wonders surrounding the birth of Jesus have most meaning to you?

____ God became human in Christ Jesus.

____ Jesus was born of a virgin.

____ Mary's faith was so great, she believed this would happen to her.

Which answer best describes who Jesus is for you?

____ I don't know.

____ a great teacher

____ God who became fully human

____ a savior who came to redeem broken people

____ a worker of miracles

When you think of Jesus, what quality comes first to your mind?

____ impartial loving

____ compassionate

____ kind

____ firm

____ forgiving

____ forceful

Faith and Prayer

____ What changes occur when you pray?

____ I change.

____ Little or nothing changes.

____ Circumstances change.

____ My outlook changes.

Why is prayer important in your life?

____ It serves as a powerful resource.

____ It enables me to cope.

____ It gives me what I need.

____ It helps me communicate with God.

____ It helps me see things in perspective.

When are you most likely to pray?

____ When I am frightened.

____ When someone is ill.

____ When I want something very much.

____ When I am thankful for something.

____ When I am confused.

How often do you pray?

_____ every day

_____ several times a day

_____ about once a week

_____ hardly ever

For whom do you pray most?

_____ myself

_____ my family

_____ my friends

_____ people in need whom I don't know

The Bible

To understand the Bible it is best to approach it:

_____ as a scientist.

_____ as a poet.

_____ as an historian.

_____ as a believer.

_____ as a skeptic.

The Devil

Evil's greatest victory in human fives is in convincing people:

_____ they don't need God.

_____ there is no God.

_____ it doesn't matter what faith you have.

_____ all religions have some good in them.

_____ God was invented by weak people as a crutch.

Grace
Which is grace most like?

____ God's acceptance of the past, allowing us to move into the future without guilt

____ God loving us with no strings attached

____ a reward from God

Christian Life
Which is most important to know about the membership of a church you are interested in joining?

____ its denomination

____ if it is liberal, conservative, fundamental, radical

____ if it is Christian

____ other

What season in the church year has the most meaning to your faith?

____ Pentecost

____ Advent

____ Christmas

____ Lent

____ Easter

Which is most important in your life?

____ happiness

____ security

____ success

Which is most important to you?

____ God

____ other people

____ a sense of fulfillment

Which do you think is the most difficult commandment for most people to keep? (Rank four of them only.)

____ Thou shalt have no other gods before Me.

____ Thou shalt not take the Name of the Lord thy God in vain; for the Lord will not hold him guiltless that taketh His Name in vain.

____ Remember the Sabbath day, to keep it holy.

____ Honor thy father and thy mother.

____ Thou shalt not kill.

____ Thou shalt not commit adultery.

____ Thou shalt not steal.

____ Thou shalt not bear false witness against thy neighbor.

____ Thou shalt not covet thy neighbor's house.

____ Thou shalt not covet thy neighbor's wife, nor his manservant, nor his maidservant, nor his cattle, nor anything that is thy neighbor's.

Continuum

Instructions: Pages 32-33 give purpose and procedure for the Continuum exercise.

Participants choose that place on the continuum, between two opposite extremes, which most closely represents their personal viewpoint.

General Faith Continuums

What is sin to you?

|————————————————————————————|

Sin is separation from God and need not be a part of our life.

Sin is part of human nature — we are born with sin, and everything we do is tainted with it.

How do you feel about the Christian faith as a way of life?

|———————————————————————————————|

I am skeptical of anything that tries to tell me the right way to live.

I am glad for a faith that gives my life direction.

What place does doubt have in religious faith?

|———————————————————————————————|

You must accept all religious beliefs without question.

Demand proof before you accept any religious belief.

How do you view the Bible?

|———————————————————————————————|

as a literal interpretation of God's Word

as a guide, to be individually interpreted

How do you feel about the existence of Satan?

|———————————————————————————————|

The Devil is within us.

The Devil is dead.

How free are you to affect the course of your life?

|———————————————————————————————|

Most of life is decided for us, rather than by us.

We are responsible for what happens with our lives.

When do you find faith most meaningful?

|———————————————————————————————|

When I experience it on a personal, private level.

When I share it with others.

Which is most important to you?

|———————————————————————————————|

Thou shalt!

Thou shalt not!

Either/Or

Instructions: Pages 34-35 give the purpose and procedure for the Either/Or exercise.

Participants select, between two choices, the option with which they most closely identify.

General Faith Either/Or Exercises
Faith is more like:
> believing / hoping
> action / surrender
> a miracle / a gift

The Lord's Supper is more like:
> a feast / a snack
> sorrow / joy
> one / many
> law / gospel
> command / promise
> earth / heaven

Repentance is more like:
> I can do better. / I can't do it by myself.

The Holy Spirit is more like:
> new / old
> past / present
> open / closed
> structure / no structure
> inside / outside

The main purpose of the Bible is to give people guidelines for:
> doing / knowing
> performing good acts / avoiding evil acts

Praying is more like:
>stumbling in the dark / walking in the light
>God within us / God around us
>seeing / hearing
>noise / quiet
>thanking / asking
>crying / laughing
>looking up / looking down
>outward / inward

God

Which is God more like?
>out looking for us / looking out for us

How do you understand the term "God?"
>humans projecting highest ideals / supernatural being

Love for God is more like:
>visible / invisible
>outer acts of love for people / inner devotion to God

Which do you think is most important to God?
>the beliefs we hold / the life we live

How do you see our relationship to God?
>God needs us. / We need God.

Jesus

What do you think of when you think of Jesus?
>charisma / humility
>the calm / the storm
>acceptance / rejection
>dove / hawk
>lion / lamb
>stop / go
>liberal / conservative
>intense / mild
>poor / rich
>talker / listener

doctor / teacher
loner / many friends
human / divine
lives / lived
the king / the commoner
superstar / cheerleader

Faith
Which is your faith more like?
rain / sunshine
skiing / mountain climbing
a balloon / a bowling ball
hammer / nail
a butterfly / a cocoon
a closed window / an open door
a pillow / a rock
a question / an answer
knowing / searching
mining for gold / planting a garden
trusting an old friend / making a new friend

Christian Life
Life with Christ is more like:
autumn / spring
summer / winter
a walk through woods / a walk through meadows
a pool / a river

Which best describes persons professing the Christian faith?
They are Christians. / They are Christian.

The Christian life is more:
inner-directed / outer-directed

A Christian is more like:
a candle / a mirror
asking / telling
a child / an adult

Following Christ is more like:
> costly / free
> riding / walking
> falling / climbing

Life and Death
Death is more like:
> beginning / end
> a dark closet / a sun-filled doorway
> day / night
> joy / sorrow
> a period / an exclamation mark
> closing a door / opening a door
> a friend / an enemy
> prison / lighthouse

Life is more like:
> a beating heart / an active mind
> work / play
> fire / water
> coming / going
> a journey / a home

What do you believe about life after death?
> Life goes on after death. / Death is the end.
> I have eternal life. / I'm not sure I have eternal life.

Listening

Instructions: Pages 35-37 give the purpose and procedure for the Listening exercise. Study the procedures carefully.

Participants respond to a stimulus statement in groups of three. Each person is "on focus" for five minutes.

Faith and Doubt

In class one day, Joan announced, "The Apostle Paul says that nothing — not even death — can separate us from God. This should be comforting, but it just doesn't work out that way for most of us. Harsh realities like sickness and hunger and poverty and death often do separate us from God."

In a conversation with a friend, George said, "Bill told me people should *know* that they have eternal life. How can one be that presumptuous? A person just can't know for sure."

Cathy included this statement in a letter she wrote: "It's easy to talk about God when things are going great. But I'm not really so sure any more about a God who really looks after each of us and answers our prayers. Maybe that kind of God is just a projection of our needs and hopes. Looking to God for help is just a way of kidding yourself. You really have to make it on your own."

Personal Beliefs

Chris told Andrea: "I don't remember one big moment in my life like Paul had on the road to Damascus — when God's spirit came upon him and changed his life. Some call that conversion. I know my parents baptized me and that the pastor then called me 'a child of God.' But maybe my Baptism, like Paul's conversion, was just the beginning of my growth as a Christian — like a seed that takes a long, long time to become a grain of wheat."

Mary said to Alice: "I've always believed what the Book of Proverbs says: 'Train up a child in the way he should go, and when he is old he will not depart from it.' I've always counted on that for my children. But sometimes I wonder. I can give them Christian training and set good examples, but I can't really pass my faith on. My kids must work out their own faith themselves."

Ted said: "You can never know for sure what other people think or feel about their religious faith. One person can be a faithful church member and lack assurance of eternal life. Another person can work on many church committees and have no personal relationship with Jesus Christ. On the other hand, a person who isn't active at all may have a really firm faith. You just can't tell a book by its cover."

Sharing Beliefs

Jane said to Mike: "I can't *give* faith to another person, because faith is a gift from *God*. In my own case, I didn't reach faith by studying church dogmas or by inheriting it from my parents. I helped deepen my faith by experiencing life and reflecting on my life-experience. And I can help others who are struggling with faith by listening to them, telling them what my faith means to me, and above all, living out my faith."

Mr. Johns said: "There's much Gospel in many of us. it doesn't come from the pulpit only. By sharing with one another we examine our own faith and discover we can minister to one another and help one another. The Church should find more ways to help its members do this."

Church Influence

This is what Marge had to say: "The Church is just another exclusive club. The Church requires our attendance, our money. It requires that we believe doctrines and uphold traditions. But it does not ask that we measure up to the standard of our leader Jesus Christ, who said, 'If any man would come after me, let him deny himself and take up his cross and follow me.' If the Church is serious about what it stands for, it should set stricter, higher standards."

Jim said to Tom: "The Church today really confuses me. It needs to take a stand. We must stop changing basic Christian beliefs so that they will conveniently fit today's life-style and world. Cultures may come and go, but basic Christianity must continue as Christ proclaimed it in the Gospel."

Harry responded to a neighbor's question by saying: No, I still don't belong to any church — nor do I have a faith of any kind. I've always been puzzled by those who claim to be Christians. The ones I know seem to be joyless, and yet Christianity is supposed to be a faith with joy. Christians don't seem to be any better at handling life than anyone else, and yet the Christian faith claims a kind of power. Many Christians I know seem overly anxious about life, which doesn't jibe with the Christian faith's claim of peace. And I frankly don't understand bickering and strife within a Church that proclaims love and forgiveness."

Christian Life

Rachel confided to Bruce, "Tension and anxiety really help a person be a better Christian. When I have everything I need and things are comfortable, I find it difficult to think about spiritual realities. But when the rug is pulled from under me and I encounter many problems and anxieties, then I really examine my life and question its meaning. That's when faith begins to grow! So — we should rejoice and be thankful for discomfort and pain."

Al said to his brother: "Today a girl in my class said, 'It's my life, and I can live it as I want.' But I think a real Christian always asks first of all, 'How will this action of mine affect others?' A true Christian always thinks of others before self."

After receiving a letter from his friend, Ben was puzzled; he asked: "How can this be? Art just wrote me from his work with the poor in this remote, deprived area. He says he never thinks about money and trusts God for it completely. And a check seems to arrive whenever money is needed. Now, he thinks he can depend solely on faith and live by what Jesus said: 'Don't be anxious about tomorrow.' But I don't see how a responsible person can live like that. He has to get his money some place. That means other people have to be continually supporting him."

 # Interviewing

Instructions: Pages 39-43 give purpose and procedure for the Interviewing exercise.

A volunteer from among the participants is interviewed before the group.

In addition to members of your group, you might consider a faith interview with a layperson, your pastor, a youth worker, a parent, a person in one of the trades, a doctor, a teacher, a person in any occupation.

Select appropriate questions from pages 40-41. In addition, you might want to consider these questions:

- Do you think a religious faith is an important part of life?

- Would you like to share how religion is important in your life?

- What part has your church life played in your religious faith?

- Have any church activities given you an outlet for living or practicing your religious beliefs?
- Have you experienced times when your faith was stronger than at other times? Do you think most people have periods of doubt? How do you think a person can deal with doubt?
- How would you respond to a person who asked, "Are you saved?"
- Have you had any real crises of faith? Are you more like a person who has found the answers, or like a person who is still searching? Is there anything that I have not asked that you'd like to comment on, or to add?

Miscellaneous Exercises

The remaining exercises in this section are one of a kind. The purpose of each is to help participants further examine what they believe and value about their faith. Procedures are given for each.

Interviewing Historical Figures
(Time required: 10-15 minutes)

1. Ask group members to review the life and thought of an historical figure such as Saint Paul, Saint Thomas Aquinas, Martin Luther, Mary Baker Eddy, Saint Theresa.

2. Either you or another group member can conduct an interview with the figure chosen; for example, with Saint Paul. Have one person answer as Paul might have answered. Interview Paul to find out about turning points in his life, his faith and particular beliefs, why he did certain things.

Who Is Jesus?
(Time required: 20-30 minutes)
Jesus said: I am . . .
> the Good Shepherd   John 10:14

---

the Bread of Life	John 6:35, 48, 51
the Way	John 14:6
the Truth	John 14:6
the Life	John 14:6
the Door	John 10:9
the Resurrection	John 11:25-26
the True Vine	John 15:5
Teacher	John 13:13
Lord	John 13:13

Give the following instructions:

1. Share your answers to the following questions in groups of four:

   • Does one of these "I am's" mean more to you than the others? If so, explain.

   • How does it help you know who Jesus is?

   • Do you learn anything about yourself as you think about who Jesus is? If so, what?

2. Think for a few minutes about who you are. Complete the statement "I am . . ." with six different responses.

3. Share your "I am. . ." completions with a partner. What does your own religious experience have to do with these answers?

4. Pretend your partner does not know Jesus, and you do. Introduce Jesus to your partner. Tell him or her who Jesus is to you personally.

Definition of Faith
(Time required: 15-20 minutes)

1. Give the following instructions: "In groups of 4, think of the word *faith*. Brainstorm definitions of faith — as many as you can think of — whatever occurs to you. Write them down quickly. Don't evaluate them yet."

2. Ask each group to reach a consensus on one definition.

3. Now reassemble the total group. Compile one list from all groups.

4. Ask the total group to consider these questions: Is there a common theme that runs through these definitions? Did you discover any new insights into the definition of faith? What are they? Do they clarify your definition? How?

Faith Shield

This exercise gives individuals an opportunity to think about the characteristics of their own personal faith and to depict their faith experiences on a personal Faith Shield. (Time required: 20-30 minutes)

1. Reproduce the Faith Shield shown on page 73, or ask each participant to make a facsimile of the shield.
2. Have participants fill in each section of the Faith Shield by drawing a picture, symbol, or design in the designated area to represent their responses. (Written words are acceptable if response is difficult to translate pictorially.) Give the following instructions:
   - In section A, depict the key ingredient of your faith.
   - In section B, depict an action you once took because of your religious faith.
   - In section C, depict a person who was important in the development of your faith.
   - In section D, depict one thing that sometimes interferes with your living your faith.
   - In section E, depict one belief about which you are very certain.
   - In section F, write or depict three words that describe your faith.
3. Have participants share, in groups of 4, the drawings on their shields, explaining to each other the meanings behind the symbols. (A sharing option is to post all shields, having them available for everyone to see.)

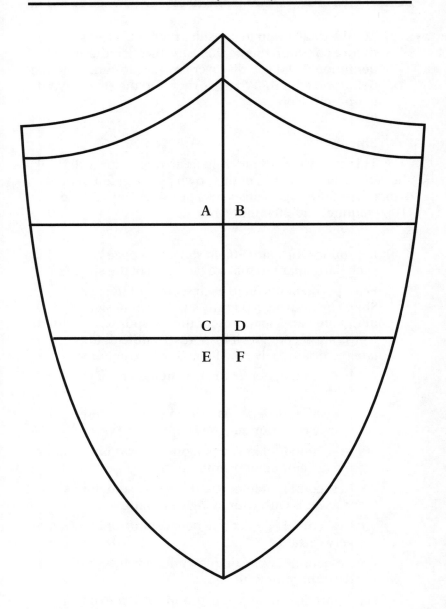

Permission is given to reproduce this page for group and family use.

Sharing Faith
(Time required: 15-20 minutes)

1. Read the following to the group: "Terry, a high school senior, said, 'I know Christ and value my relationship with him so I want others to know him too.' His method was to confront another person with the question, 'Are you saved?'

2. Ask participants to think about how they share their faith. Then brainstorm, with the group, as. many possibilities as you can, writing them on a chalkboard.

3. Ask the group to consider which of the ways listed might have the most influence on them.

4. Have participants consider, in groups of 4, the following questions:

   - If you wished to communicate something about your own faith, which way would be most comfortable for you?

   - Is there a "best" way? (Groups might try role playing each of these ways.)

   - Can you reach a consensus of two or three effective ways?

   - Is it impossible to argue anyone into the Christian faith? Explain.

5. Reassemble total group and share learnings.

Archibald's Experiment
(Time required: 30-40 minutes)

Archibald is a college student who is confused about his faith. He was brought up in a Christian home but rejected Christianity as a teenager. He now takes great pride in telling others that he is an atheist. However, he is curious about how people express faith and is writing a term paper — due in three days — on the subject. In order to get people to open up, he decides to *pretend* he is interested in changing. He goes to see the college chaplain who has been trying for two years to talk with Archibald about conversion.

The chaplain is glad to see Archibald and listens to his false tale. The chaplain tells Archibald that he will be able to solve all his future problems by believing and putting his trust in the Lord. When Archibald begins to ask some questions, the chaplain explains that he can't spend any more time with him that day, because he has promised to meet a friend at the golf course. Archibald tells him that it's very important and that he needs a couple of hours right away. The chaplain promises to meet with him after the weekend, spending as much time as necessary then.

After leaving the chaplain, Archibald calls Candy and asks if he can come over because there's something important on his mind. Candy was raised as a Christian, but she is not too sure of her beliefs. Recently, she began a meditation course and has found meditation to be a positive force in her life. She assures Archibald that meditation is just what he needs, ignoring Archibald's apparent desire to return to the Church. She adds, "A lot of that stuff they teach you at church just isn't worth anything."

The next morning, Archibald goes to see his friend Dr. Leroy, who is taking a day's vacation from his dental practice. Dr. Leroy gladly agrees to spend any time needed with Archibald. After hearing what Archibald has to say, Dr. Leroy points out that it's really not important what you believe, just so you believe something. He adds: "All religions are the same as far as I am concerned. I go to church myself every Sunday. Actually, it's been good for my practice. Most of the people in our church have their dental work done at my office. join us next Sunday if you'd like to try it out."

Continuing to pretend, Archibald calls a former Sunday school teacher, Mrs. Davis. He takes Mrs. Davis to dinner that night so that he will have enough time to collect plenty of information for his paper. She is thrilled at his possible change of heart and can hardly contain her enthusiasm. Archibald barely has a chance to tell her of his interest in returning to the fold, when she begins telling him how she has disapproved of his actions in the past and what he should do to change his life. Archibald has lots of questions, but doesn't have a chance to ask them because Mrs. Davis is so busy admonishing him to read the Bible, pray every day, and change his behavior.

1. Read the story aloud; then have the total group split into groups of 5 or 6.

2. Ask the groups to rank the characters from best to worst and then to share their rankings with each other.

3. Ask the groups to make a consensus ranking.

4. After about 15 minutes, have each group report their consensus if they reached one.

5. You might wish to tabulate on the chalkboard the "best" person and the "worst" person choices of all participants using the following format:

	Best Person	Worst Person
Archibald		
Chaplain		
Candy		
Dr. Leroy		
Mrs. Davis		

6. Invite any brief statements by participants.

7. Have small groups discuss how people can be most helpful to another person who is searching for meaning in life and using them as a resource.

Faith Questions
(Time required: 25-30 minutes)

1. Ask each person to write down two questions he or she has about the Christian faith.

2. Divide the group into pairs. Have pairs designate person A and person B in each.

3. Explain that in each pair, person A will ask person B one question, and person B will answer to the best of

his or her ability. Then person B will ask one question, and person A will answer. This procedure is repeated. (Set a time limit of 10 minutes.)

4. When each pair has completed their questions and answers, ask all A's to remain seated while B's select a new partner. Repeat the asking and answering process described above. (This can be repeated with yet another partner.)

5. Reassemble the group and ask them to share one thing they learned.
   Optional: Have the large group place all their questions in a box. Immediately (or at a later time in the session), ask your priest, minister, or some knowledgeable layperson for an interview. Use the questions from the group as the basis for the interview.

Faith Celebration

Easter — New Life
(Time required: approximately 35-40 minutes)

1. Have everyone in your family or group list the feeling words they associate with Good Friday and the feeling words they associate with Easter.

2. Ask participants the following questions:
   • At what time in your life have you had Good Friday feelings?
   • Have you had a time when you moved from Good Friday feelings to Easter feelings?

3. Have participants share their responses with another person or in a group of 4.

4. Now ask participants to spend a few minutes thinking about Jesus Christ, his death and Resurrection. Ask:
   • What does Jesus' Resurrection mean to you?
   • How might your life be different if Jesus had not risen?

5. Ask the group to reflect in silence.

6. After this time of silence, ask the group to find some way to express their thoughts about Jesus. Give these suggestions: "Look around the room for an object, take a walk outdoors, create something, write a poem or a song. Let your imagination go. After 10-15 minutes, return to the group and share your creativity and findings."

7. After sharing, have the group think of a special way to celebrate Easter.

Three Levels of Learning

Give Me the Facts! (See Hebrews 11)
Questions to answer:

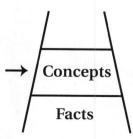

- How is faith defined in Hebrews 11?

- List the examples of faith noted in this chapter.

- What people were involved?

- What did they do that illustrated the kind of faith they had?

- What was their goal? (Hebrews 11:14-16)

- Why, according to the writer of

- Hebrews, did they not receive all that was promised to them?

What's the Idea?
Concepts to explore:

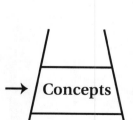

- What were the results of their faith?

- What characteristics within them enabled them to go out in faith?

- What kind of a relationship did they have with God?
- List some contemporary people who exemplify faith. What did they do that made them outstanding examples of faith?
- Can their deeds be matched with some of the words used of the people in Hebrews 11?
- What might the writer have meant by "God had foreseen something better for us?"

What's In It for Me?
Valuing suggestions:

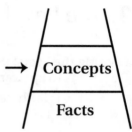

- Give your definition of faith. Do the words "obey," "trust," "believe," "vision," "courage" say anything to you about your faith?
- Compare your relationship to God with those of the Old Testament people of faith. Are some of their characteristics of faith also in your relationship with God? Which ones? Are some missing? Which ones? Is God calling you to some special task today?
- How can you strengthen your faith? Think of something specific you can do about it. Set a goal that will lead you in that direction.
- Share some of the feelings about your faith with another person.

Resources from the Bible
(for optional use)

God

Genesis 1	"In the beginning God . . . ."
Job 38:1-7	"Where were you. . .?"
1 Kings 19:9-12	The hidden God.
Psalm 104	God the Creator
Isaiah 40:12-31	No words can describe God.
Romans 11:33	A great God.
Psalm 139:1-10	God searches for his people.
Romans 1:19-20	God makes himself known to people.
John 12:44	Jesus declares God as the authority.
Ephesians 4:6	One Lord — one God.

Faith — What Is It?

Hebrews 11:1	Faith defined.
Hebrews 11	Faith of Old Testament figures.
Genesis 12:1-8	Abraham obeyed.
Genesis 22:1-10	Abraham is tested.
Exodus 14:21-31	Crossing the Red Sea.
Psalm 14:1	To the fool there is no God.
Mark 4:35-41	Why have you no faith?
Matthew 17:14-21	Faith to move mountains.
John 20:24-29	Honest doubt.
Luke 1:26-38	Mary believes she is to bear the Savior.
2 Corinthians 5:6-10	By faith, not by sight.
James 2:14-18	Faith and works.
Romans 3:20-26 and Galatians 3:23-26	Justified by faith.
Ephesians 2:8	Faith, a gift from God.
Mark 9:24	"I believe; help my unbelief!"
Romans 10:17	Faith by hearing the preaching of Christ.

Life and Teachings of Jesus
Matthew
Mark
Luke
John

Who Is Jesus?

Isaiah 9:6	"Wonderful, Counselor, Mighty God, Everlasting Father, Prince of Peace."
Isaiah 53	"A man of sorrows."
Matthew 7:24-29	Jesus speaks with authority.
Matthew 1:21	'Jesus. "
Matthew 1:23	"Emmanuel."
Luke 31-36	'Jesus." "Son of the Most High." "Son of God."
John 1:1-5	"The Word."
John 1:14	"Word made flesh."
John 1:29	"Lamb of God."
John 4:42	"Savior of the World."
John 6:35	"Bread of Life."
John 7:12	"Light of the World."
John 10	"The Good Shepherd."
John 11	"The Resurrection and the Life."
John 14:6-7	"The Way, the Truth, the Life."
John 15:5	"The Vine."
Matthew 16:16	"Christ, Son of the Living God."

Christian Life

Galatians 2:15-21	Life lived in faith.
Romans 5	Faith in Christ makes us friends with God.
Romans 8	A healthy spiritual fife.
Ephesians	New life in Christ.
Philippians	Joy.
1 Corinthians 12	Spiritual gifts.
1 Corinthians 13	Faith, Hope, Love.
2 Timothy 1:2	"I know whom I have believed."
Matthew 10:39	Cost of following Christ.

Sharing Faith

Matthew 28:16-20	Tell others — to all the world.
Romans 1:16-17	Sharing the Good News.
Romans 10:9-10	Tell others that Jesus is Lord.

Prayer

Matthew 14:23	Jesus prayed.
Psalm 50:15	God hears prayer.
Luke 11:1-13	"Teach us to pray."
Matthew 6:5-15	"When you pray.
Matthew 5:44	Pray for enemies.
Matthew 7:7-8	Ask, seek, knock.
Matthew 18:19-20	Promise to answer prayer requests.
Matthew 21:22	Ask in faith.
Luke 18:10-14	Two men praying in the Temple.
Romans 8:26-27	The Holy Spirit helps us pray.
Ephesians 6:18	"Pray at all times in the Spirit."
James 5:13-16	Results of prayer.

Life — Death

John 5:24	Eternal life begins now.
Job 19:25	"I know that my Redeemer lives."
Matthew 28:20	"I am with you always."
Psalm 23	"The Lord is my Shepherd."
1 Thessalonians 4:13	Christians have hope.
Romans 8:38-39	Nothing separates us from God.
Romans 12:15	Empathy with others.
Philippians 1:19-26	Paul's dilemma — death, or life?
John 14:1-7	"Let not your hearts be troubled.
John 14:18-19	"Because I live, you will live."
Romans 14:7	In life or death we belong to God.

Death Is Conquered — Christ Lives

John 11
Romans 5
1 Corinthians 15
2 Corinthians 4
Revelations 5 and 7

Holy Spirit

John 14:25-31	Promise of the Holy Spirit.
John 16:13-14	Spirit of Truth.
John 3:5-8	Born of the Spirit.
Luke 11:13	Asking for the Holy Spirit.
Acts 1:8	Power promised.
Acts 2:1-13	Tongues of fire.
Book of Acts	Work of the Holy Spirit in the early Church.
2 Corinthians 1:21-22	God's guarantee.
Galatians 5:22-23	Fruit of the Spirit.

The Trinity
Matthew 28:19
Romans 5:1-8
2 Corinthians 13:14

Word of God

Romans 10:17	Faith comes from hearing the Word.
Hebrews 4:12	Word of God is "living and active."
Psalm 119:11	God's Word in the human heart.
Psalm 119:105	"A lamp unto my feet."
John 8:31	"Truth will make you free."
1 Corinthians 1:18	The Word — folly, or power?

Baptism
Matthew 28:19-20
John 1:33
Ephesians 4:5
Colossians 2:12
1 Peter 3:21-22
Romans 6:1-11

The Lord's Supper
Matthew 26:20-29
Mark 14:17-25
Luke 22:14-23
John 13:21-30
1 Corinthians 11:17-34

Prayer

Lord, I have said "Yes" to you. I love you! I believe in you and am sure of your love — a love that followed me every time I tried to run away. I no longer want to run away, but every once in awhile I still cry out, "I believe, Lord; help my unbelief!"

Thank you for the people who touch my life and encourage me in my faith. Thank you for forgiving and loving me so much you were willing to die on the cross for me. May your own constant trust and obedience, even in the most trying times, be a model and an inspiration for me.

Valuing My Family

We are optimistic about the family's potential, for we firmly believe that family life can provide a unique climate for individual and group growth and support.

But family life is not easy these days. Each family member must make many value-laden choices — choices which frequently involve the entire family. Communication is often difficult and conflicts become a part of every family's experience. The crucial question is: How do we handle these difficulties?

We think that people can profit from greater in-depth discussions with their own family members as well as with persons from other families. They need to practice listening to one another, developing sensitivity to diverse viewpoints.

These exercises provide a chance for family members to examine their own ideas, to listen to one another, to understand each other, and to grow in mutual respect. The result is often greater peace, joy, and harmony.

The exercises can be used:

- at group meetings in which parents and children collect in family units to complete the exercises.
- at group meetings in which only individuals (not families) are present.
- at home, with one's own family.

In general, the directions for exercises are written for group meetings at which a number of families are present. For other uses, modification in procedures might be necessary.

Before using this chapter, please review the chapter on leadership.

Voting

Instructions: Pages 30-31 give purpose and procedure for the a Voting exercises.

Participants vote in the following manner:

Agree?	(Raise hand.)
Strongly agree?	(Wave hand.)
Disagree?	(Thumb down.)
Strongly disagree?	(Shake thumb.)
Pass?	(Fold arms across chest.)

General Voting Questions on Family

How many of you:

- would like to develop more family unity but don't know how?
- think family size should be limited?
- see the Church as a family?
- think children should interact with grandparents as much as possible?
- think family members should share in decision making?
- think the family, as a unit, will survive?
- think many couples are unprepared for marriage?
- think the Church should help more to prepare people for marriage?
- think the Church should do more to help family members listen to one another?
- think Christian faith stabilizes families?
- think devotions -should be a part of everyday family life?
- wish you could share your faith more easily with your family?

Marriage

How many of you:

- think there are alternate kinds of marriage permissible for Christians?

- would approve of contract marriages in which the contract would come up for renewal every few years?

- wish you know (or had known) more about what to look for in a mate?

- would like to know more about marriage?

- have read a book on marriage within the last year?

- think a marriage built on long-term friendship is the strongest?

- think the rate of marriage breakdowns in the over-forty age bracket is alarming?

- think that living together before marriage can be a good way to test a relationship?

- think that sexuality today is viewed in a more positive way than ever before?

- think that how people live and develop their sexuality is their own business?

- think the Church should do more to help persons deal

- with themselves as sexual beings?

- think that one person can meet all or most of another person's human needs?

- would marry someone from a different race?

- would marry someone from a different ethnic group?

- would marry someone from a different religion?

- are concerned about the divorce rate?

- know of a separation or divorce that worked out best for everyone?

- know of a separation or divorce that caused more harm than good?

- think that both partners are always responsible for a broken marriage?

- think young people are not trying hard enough to make their marriages work?
- think teenage marriages usually end in divorce?
- think most couples marry too young?
- think divorce is sinful according to traditional Christian teaching?
- think a Christian should not marry a non-Christian?
- think people who do not marry in their early twenties usually do not marry at all?

Role of Husband and Wife
How many of you agree with this statement?

- The woman's traditional role of wife and mother should be given priority over any position outside the home.
- A father should have as much responsibility for raising the children as the mother.
- The feminist movement frequently contributes to breakdown in marriages.
- The feminist movement has strengthened marriage.
- "As the Church is subject to Christ, so let wives be subject in everything to their husbands." (Ephesians 5:24)
- No-fault divorce laws contribute to the breakdown of marriages.
- The husband should have the final say in the home.
- Husband and wife should share authority equally.
- A woman's obedience to her husband can weaken her own authority.
- The family needs one person as the recognized final authority.
- Most women are proud of a husband who will assume the role of leadership and authority in the home.

How many of you:

- think a woman's place is in the home? work outside your home? are happy in your work?
- are housewives but feel you should also be working outside your home? are spending a lot of time working outside your home but would like more time at home?
- think your home life is enhanced by a job outside the home?
- think women make better single parents than men?
- think freedom for women means freedom for men?

Parenting

How many of you:

- think most young people take their problems to their parents?
- think communication is more open in families today than in the past?
- think the moral character of youth is declining?
- think the moral character of adults is declining?
- think that the family's view of a child greatly influences the child's view of himself or herself?
- think children should share their joys, fears, and problems with their parents?
- think parents should share their joys, fears, and problems with their children? would like to air more problems in the family?
- think that all of your family members feel they actually share in making decisions?
- look (or looked) to your parents for help in making decisions?
- think parents tend to underestimate the abilities of their children?
- think children should have some say in the way family money is spent? think many parents hesitate to guide

their children in religious matters because their own beliefs are not clear? think most young people have trouble talking about their beliefs?

- think most parents have trouble talking about their beliefs? have been strongly influenced by your parents? confide in a member of your family?

- feel comfortable telling your parents your personal problems?

- wish you could be a happier person in your home? think your parents have helped you understand yourself? think children should have to work for an allowance? would (or do) raise your own children more strictly than you were raised?

- think parents should be totally consistent in handling family matters?

- think a fifteen-year-old should obey his or her parents even if the parents' best reason seems to be "because I said so?"

- think young people today are spoiled?

- think a breakdown in family relationships contributes to teenage drug abuse?

- think parents should always try to understand the child's point of view, no matter how different from their own?

- think that being close friends with their parents is good for children?

- wish there were more children in your family?

- will never spank your children?

- were sometimes spanked when you were young? agree that if one member of a family hurts, then all hurt?

- think a good family life once shielded many teens from trouble?

Church Influence

How many of you:

- see the Church as a family?
- think that exclusive concern for your own church family can stunt your church's growth?
- think the total congregation should do more things together?
- think your church is a community of people who really care about one another?
- wish more people would talk to one another at church?
- wish there were more opportunities to work together as a family within the church family?
- think that at worship it's important to mention the names of people in need?
- think the sexual freedom and sexual attitudes of our society can be clearly labeled as Christian or un-Christian?
- think a church should not allow discussion of matters such as homosexuality, masturbation, and premarital sex?
- think Christian churches should avoid sex education?
- think that the Church should speak out on issues that affect family life, such as abortion and divorce?
- think the Church should do more to educate families and parents about sex, marriage, and family fife?
- think the Church should initiate programs and activities to strengthen family life?
- think that, in the long run, family life is often fragmented by the Church?
- would want your own children to have the same kind of church life you had as a youngster?
- think the Church ignores single adults?
- think the Church is a lonely place if you're not married?

How many of you agree with the following statement?

- The Church could easily and satisfactorily substitute as a family for those who either have no families or who live alone.
- The Christian faith is the best foundation on which to build a satisfying family life.

Family Traditions

How many of you:

- love to celebrate special family occasions?
- think it's important to keep up traditional celebrations like Christmas and birthdays?
- think traditional family celebrations are unimportant?
- like to be remembered on your birthday with a celebration?
- think celebrating is a bother?
- have recently begun a family tradition?
- exchange gifts at Christmas?
- received gifts on your last birthday?
- think traditional celebrations have become too commercialized? think giving gifts is a pleasure? think giving gifts is overdone?
- think sending Christmas cards is a tradition that has lost its meaning? like to create your own cards as a family? think Christmas is a lonely time of year? celebrated last Christmas in much the same way you did when you were a small child?
- have ever shared your Christmas Eve supper with someone who was lonely?
- rarely give to needy people except at Christmas?
- think the Christmas spirit has diminished?

Family and Social Issues
How many of you: have worked together as a family on a social issue?

- think your parents are well informed on social issues?
- know what others in your family think about current issues?
- wish your family were more interested in social issues?
- are aware of your parents helping others in need?
- agree with your family on most political issues?
- think it's difficult getting your family to work together?

Ranking

Instructions: Pages 31-32 give purpose and procedure for the Ranking exercise.

Participants rank all items in order of preference or priority (1 = most important; 2 = next most important, etc.).

General Family Rankings
Which is most important in family life?

____ sharing

____ loyalty

____ respect

Which is the most important in family life?

____ fidelity

____ love

____ discipline

Which is the most important factor in a successful family?

____ husband or wife with a good job

____ mother who remains in the home

____ regular church attendance

____ love among family members

Which has had the greatest influence on your religious beliefs?

____ parents and family

____ friends

____ teachers, clergy

____ personal experiences

Which should the Christian family be most concerned about?

____ service

____ love

____ personal growth

What best characterizes a Christian family?

____ caring for one another

____ forgiving one another

____ spiritual commitment

____ acceptance of one another

What is the best way to share your religious faith with your family?

____ sharing Christian books

____ living the faith

____ encouraging the family to attend church

____ leading family devotions

Marriage

What do you see as the greatest obstacle to a successful marriage?

_____ unfaithfulness

_____ careless use of money

_____ career ambition

_____ lack of common interests

Which is the most important characteristic in a mate?

_____ thoughtfulness

_____ strength

_____ gentleness

What communication skill do you most value in your mate?

_____ ability to articulate ideas

_____ ability to listen

_____ ability to understand your feelings

Which kind of marriage do you think holds the greatest promise for satisfaction and happiness?

_____ marriage with a renewable contract

_____ traditional marriage

_____ open marriage

Which would you rather do?

_____ Review our present marriage contract to see what each of us expected to give and receive when we got married.

_____ Renegotiate the marriage contract to meet our present needs.

_____ Leave things as they are.

Which of these men do you disagree with most?

____ John said, "A woman's place is in the home.

____ Working women deprive their husbands and children of certain family relationships. They are too tired at the end of the day."

____ Joe said, "Behind every successful man there's a woman."

____ Archie said, "When a wife greets her husband at the door after he's put in a hard day at work, she should be freshly scrubbed and have a cheery, positive attitude."

Parenting

Which is the greatest influence on a child's life today?

____ church

____ home

____ school

____ friends

____ television

What do parents most need to effectively raise their children?

____ common sense

____ special training in parenting

____ adequate help from school and church

What is the most important parental characteristic?

____ consistency

____ fairness

____ acceptance

What is the main goal of parenting?

____ to raise obedient children

____ to provide for the children

____ to help the children become independent

____ to foster mutual respect between parent and child

You are a parent. Which problem would be hardest for you to work out with your child?

____ dropping out of high school

____ sexual promiscuity

____ shoplifting

____ running away from home

____ drug or alcohol abuse

You are a high school sophomore. Which would be the most difficult problem to talk over with your parents?

____ You want to quit school.

____ Your steady is pressuring you to become sexually involved.

____ Your use of alcohol/drugs has gotten out of control.

As a parent, which quality in a teenager most disturbs you?

____ disobedience

____ irresponsibility

____ preoccupation with self

____ conformity to peers

As a teenager, which quality in a parent bugs you the most?

____ nagging

____ pressuring

____ lack of interest

____ inability to see your point of view

When are parents most apt to interfere?

____ in the selection of a mate

____ in child-rearing decisions

____ in educational choices

____ in the choice of life-style

What do you do when your child is being bullied?

____ tell the child to fight back

____ talk with the bullys parents

____ allow child to handle it

____ ignore it

What do youth want most from adults?

____ They want respect.

____ They want to be heard.

____ They want to participate in decision-making.

____ They want honesty.

In getting children to take responsibility, which parent would you agree with most?

____ Parent A rewards children for obedience; punishes children for disobedience.

____ Parent B allows children to make mistakes; says that's how children learn.

____ Parent C avoids conflict; ignores or tolerates behavior problems.

Church Influence

Whom does the Church influence most?

____ young children

____ teenage youth

____ adults

____ elderly

The Church could be more helpful to families by:

____ offering sex education.

____ sponsoring social service projects.

____ helping family members communicate.

____ offering preparation for marriage.

What aspect of the Church has had the most influence on your family?

_____ worship

_____ Bible study

_____ music

_____ recreational activities

Family Traditions

What time of the year do you enjoy most with your family?

_____ Easter

_____ Christmas

_____ Thanksgiving

Which Christmas project might your family enjoy most?

_____ making Christmas cards together

_____ finding and decorating the Christmas tree together

_____ baking Christmas cookies together

_____ caroling together

Which do you remember with the most fondness?

_____ a family trip

_____ a family celebration

_____ a family reunion

Which would be the best vacation for your family?

_____ a camping trip

_____ a sight-seeing trip

_____ visiting special places of interest near home

Which do you enjoy most with your family?

____ picnics

____ attending shows

____ participating in sports

____ music

Which do you wish your family had more of?

____ sense of togetherness

____ greater support for one another in crises

____ humor

____ common interests

What do you like least at mealtime?

____ everyone eating at different times

____ fighting

____ hurrying

____ silence

How often do you attend church as a family?

____ almost always

____ never

____ occasionally

Family and Social Issues
A forty-five-year-old woman, with a grown family, becomes pregnant. What do you think is her best course of action?

____ to have the child and keep it

____ to have the child and give it up

____ to have an abortion

Whom would you prefer as next-door neighbors?

____ an elderly couple

____ a young couple with a mentally retarded child

____ a family of a different race from yours

____ a group of young singles

Which might your family prefer to do?

____ support an orphan

____ visit sick persons

____ raise money for the needy

Dinner Table Rankings

What bothers you most?

____ shoplifting

____ pushing drugs

____ careless driving

What do you think is most harmful to the human body?

____ cigarettes

____ marijuana

____ alcohol

____ sleeping pills

____ tranquilizers

Which chore would you prefer to do?

____ housecleaning

____ repair work

____ cooking

____ laundry

If you found a wallet, which would you do?

____ keep the money and put the wallet in a postal box

____ return the wallet to its owner

____ keep the money and throw away the wallet

Which would be the greatest loss to you?

____ eyesight

____ hearing

____ speech

Which of these subjects makes the most interesting reading?

____ world events

____ famous people

____ sports

Which would you most like to be?

____ an astronaut

____ a deep-sea diver

____ a balloonist

Which person do you think has the most challenging job?

____ an athletic coach

____ an engineer

____ a business executive

____ a nurse

____ a machinist

How would you choose to spend your spare time?

____ alone

____ with one or two friends

____ with a group

Which do you think is worst?

_____ to be punished by a teacher

_____ to have friends make fun of you

_____ to get poor grades on a report card

Which is the most enjoyable?

_____ reading a good book

_____ playing a game

_____ working a puzzle

Which would you rather use?

_____ hands

_____ mind

_____ body

Which do you prefer?

_____ movies

_____ radio

_____ TV

Which are you most likely to use as an escape at times?

_____ television

_____ drugs or alcohol

_____ work

_____ religion

_____ recreation

_____ solitude

Continuum

Instructions: Pages 32-33 give the purpose and procedure for the Continuum exercise.

Participants choose that place on the continuum, between two opposite extremes, which most closely represents their personal viewpoint.

General Family Continuums

How long should a marriage contract last?

|——————————————————————————————————|

forever;   three-year marriage contract;
can never be broken   reassess every three years.
under any circumstances.

How willing are you to forgive in your family?

|——————————————————————————————————|

always   seldom

How dependent are you on your family?

|——————————————————————————————————|

totally dependent   totally independent

How important are traditions in your family?

|——————————————————————————————————|

very important   not important

To what extent should the Church be involved in sex education?

|——————————————————————————————————|

not at all   much more

Role of Husband and Wife

Who should have the final authority in the home?

|——————————————————————————————————|

husband   wife

What do you think about working wives?

A woman's place is in the home, and women should be proud to be homemakers. Their families suffer if they aren't there every day.	A woman should have a job outside the home. She can probably do more for her family and herself by working.

Parenting

To what extent should a parent influence a child's values?

Parents should influence children's values as much as possible or they'll never learn to live decent lives. Telling children what to value is the best policy.	Parents should leave children alone to develop their own values. In fact, they should try to disguise their own values so as not to influence their children.

Who should select a child's friends?

Parents should choose the friends.	Children should choose their own friends.

How do you think children should be raised?

strictly	permissively

Either/Or

Instructions: Pages 34-35 give the purpose and procedure for Either/Or exercises.

Participants select, between two choices, the option with which they most closely identify.

General Family Either/Or Exercises

Which seems more important in family life?
  happy relationships / knowledge of the Christian faith
  tradition / change
  spirit of the Gospel / spirit of the law

In your family, which are you more like?
  giver / taker
  strict / permissive
  listener / talker
  leader / follower
  arguing / agreeing
  thinking / doing
  coach / team member
  yes / no
  jeans / dress slacks
  today /tomorrow

Which is your family more like?
  birds in a nest / bees in a hive
  live and learn / look before you leap
  purse strings / boot straps
  sweet and sour / moonlight and roses
  meat and potatoes / yogurt and granola
  a camper / a motel
  chess / spin the bottle
  rock groups / string ensemble

Parenting

Rules are most effective when they are set by:
  parents alone / parents and children together

Children need love most when they:
  get a poor report card / break a neighbor's window

Would you rather face parenthood in the middle:
  1970s / 1980s

In communicating your love to family members, which is more important?

    tell them / show them

Church Influence

It is more important to spend time in:

    church activities / family activities

The influence of the Church tends to make husband and wife:

    more equal / less equal

Which best describes the influence of church activities on the family?

    pulling together / pulling apart

Marriage

Which married couples tend to be happier?

    those with children / those without children

Which are young people more concerned about?

    career / marriage

In marriage, which is more important between mates?

    friendship / romance

Family and Social Issues

If a new family moved into your neighborhood, what would you most likely do?

    call on them / wait for them to drop in

Married couples should have:

    more children / fewer children

Listening

Instructions: Pages 35-37 give purpose and procedure for the Listening exercise. Study the procedures carefully.

Participants respond to a stimulus statement in groups of three. Each person is "on focus" for five minutes.

Church Influence

Orville said, "The Church has been too timid about discussing male-female relationships. The Church should listen to human needs and help interpret them in the light of Christ's message. The Church is the place to introduce sex education courses and premarital counseling. The Church community needs to have a warm, loving, healing atmosphere where its people can experience healthy interaction and develop close bonds without endangering marriage ties."

Frank said, "Churches today are just too liberal regarding male-female relationships. The Church's traditional approach has withstood the test of time; God's authority and history make it clear what marriage should be. The tendency to accept diverse life-styles and moods of the moment will ultimately harm family life and interfere with the effective rearing of children. The Church knows what is right and should put people on the right track. We can't be wishy-washy on this matter."

Parenting

Mrs. Evans said, "A father's word should be absolute law in a family. Whatever the father says must be obeyed without question. Children have to be trained early so they really understand this and can follow the Bible's teaching: 'Children, obey your parents in the Lord, for this is right.'

Tim, a young adult, said, "Families usually feel powerless when they try to combat drug abuse in their own children. But families could do a lot more than they think. They can listen to their children. Most parents really don't listen. They want to listen and think they actually do. But the main thing that comes across to the kid is judgment and advice plus more judgment and advice!"

At lunchtime, Harley said to the fellows at work, "Things are too easy for kids these days. Nothing is demanded of them anymore. Young people need and want direction and guidance. We adults are making a big mistake by not giving it to them. Parents and other adults should set higher standards. We need to discipline kids — let them know who's boss."

A parent said, "I hate to hear my kids quarreling. I know it's part of growing up, but it's one of the most irritating parts of being a parent. I know I sometimes confuse and puzzle them by yelling at them and condemning them for their actions. But there doesn't seem to be any alternative."

Kathy said, "A lot of us subtly try to mold our children in our own image and likeness. We pretend to be liberal, pretend we want them to become themselves, but we keep downgrading their hair-styles, the music they like, the heroes they admire, the life's work they want. What's behind it is that we want them to be just like us, but we're afraid to admit we're that tyrannical."

A frustrated, middle-aged father said, "Most parents just don't have the know-how for raising children in our complex world. Nobody has taught them how, in school or elsewhere. We should have training courses which provide the knowledge and skills for being a good parent. Completion of such training courses should be an absolute requirement for expectant parents."

A teenager had this to say: "Let's say parents model concern for human beings. The child learns this, but he or she does it in a different style, maybe in a commune. The parent gets kind of sidetracked by the style, and can't see that in the commune the same kinds of values are present — real respect for the other people who live there. It'd be great if a kid could say, 'But I really do respect the things you~ve taught me. I'm just doing it a different way.' "

Mrs. Allen firmly stated to her neighbor, "It's wrong to keep a child tied to the apron strings. We mustn't do things for them; we should help them do things for themselves. If we refrain from making a child's decisions for him or her, we're helping the child learn how to make decisions wisely and boldly."

Nancy, a college junior, said to a group of adults, "Something that goes on between parents and kids my age really bothers me. The kid will just be following the parents' values but the parent can't recognize it. For example, the parents have always modeled moderation in drinking. These parents don't use drink as an escape. They use it as sort of a sharing thing — have wine for dinner and that sort of thing. The kid will pick up those values and use marijuana in the same way, but the parents can't see this because the issue of marijuana is so emotion-laden."

Dilemma

Instructions: Pages 37-39 give purpose and procedure for the Dilemma exercise.

Participants respond to a dilemma situation, exploring alternatives and consequences and finally choosing their own best solution.

Marriage

Twenty-year-old Ruth has been going steady with Herb for a year or so. She really likes him, has thought a lot about marriage, but isn't sure if he's the one. After a pleasant and fun-filled evening, Herb is silent for awhile. Then he says, "Ruth, I've been offered a job on the Coast. I'd like you to come with me. Will you marry me?" What might Ruth do?

Parenting

Your daughter started confirmation class recently. The class has been studying Genesis. Today your daughter came home upset and said, "I sure don't believe all that creation stuff." What do you say to her?

Your seven-year-old son has been playing a lot with eight-year-old Timmy, whose family recently moved into the house next door. On occasion you have heard a good deal of loud shouting and abusive language coming from their house. You have good reason to believe that the parents drink quite heavily at times. After dinner tonight your son comes to you in great excitement and says, "Hey, Mom, where are my pajamas? Timmy wants me to stay over at his house tonight and it's O.K. with his parents." What do you do?

Your eighth grader had a lot of trouble in English class last year. Today he comes home with his report card, and you comment on his improvement in English. He says, "You have to cheat to get by in that class. All the kids do it." What do you say?

Part I: Your fifteen-year-old daughter Tracy promised to be home shortly after the youth meeting, which was to be finished at 10:00 P.M. You know she had planned to study for a biology test tomorrow. By 11:00 P.M. you are getting panicky. There is no word from Tracy. What might you do?

Part II: You are sitting in the kitchen, waiting. At 12:10 the door opens and you hear Tracy tip-toeing up the stairs to her bedroom. What do you do?

Six-year-old Michelle returns from school after a month in first grade. She is unusually quiet. The next morning after breakfast she cries and says, "I'm not going to school today." What do you do?

Nine-year-old Bill frequently fights with his older brother and sister. You pull him away as he is hitting and scrapping with them again. Bill says, "You're always blaming me when they really started it. Why don't you punish them, too? You just like them better than you like me!" What do you do?

Your son, a bright, active, and motivated high school senior, has been considering a number of colleges. He comes to you one evening to talk. You are disappointed to hear him say, "Ive decided against college." What do you say to him?

Your fifteen-year-old son Joe has been attending Sunday school regularly since age four. Lately he has been very unhappy about Sunday school, and two weeks ago he asked if he could quit because he was "not learning anything."

You said, "No. I expect all of our family to attend."

Sunday morning your entire family is getting ready to go to Sunday school classes. You are almost ready to leave when you discover Joe sitting in his room in his pajamas. He says, "I'm not going to Sunday school today or ever again." What can you do?

Interviewing

Instructions: Pages 39-43 give purpose and procedure for the Interviewing exercise.

A volunteer from among the participants is interviewed before the group.

In addition to members of your group, you might consider an interview with a middle-aged couple, a senior citizen, an engaged couple, your pastor, a youth worker, a divorced person, a marriage counselor, a social worker.

Select appropriate questions from pages 40-41. In addition, you might want to consider these questions:

- What do you think is the difference between a Christian family and a non-Christian family?
- How long have you been married?
- When did you first meet each other?
- How long did you go together before being married?
- What do you think has been responsible for the higher rate of marriage breakups?
- How do you view divorce?
- Do you think it is important for husband and wife to have the same religious faith?
- Has your religious faith made a difference in your married life together? How?
- In marriages you have seen break up, what is often the cause?
- Could some of these breakups have been prevented?
- Do you have advice for youth today?
- In your experience, what is important in a happy marriage?
- Do you have children?
- Have children enriched your marriage?
- Has your relationship with your spouse changed during your married life?

Goal Setting

Instructions: Pages 42-45 give purpose and procedure for the Goal Setting exercise.

Participants, individually, select a goal they wish to achieve, make a commitment to achieving that goal, and report their successful accomplishment of it.

You may have seen a change or two you would like to make in your family life — a change you could help bring about. Why not construct and sign a contract that will help you set a goal in the direction you want to go.

To strengthen my family life, I will ...

_____
(signature)

permission is given to reproduce this page for group and family use.

You may have seen a change you would like to make to strengthen your marriage — a change you could help bring about. Why not construct and sign a contract that will help you set a goal in the direction you want to go.

To make our marriage stronger, I will ...

_____

(signature)

permission is given to reproduce this page for group and family use.

Miscellaneous Exercises

The remaining exercises in this section are one of a kind. The purpose of each is to help participants further examine what they believe and value about the family. Procedures are given for each.

Heart Attack

This exercise gives family members an opportunity to examine their life-styles and priorities when illness strikes a member of the family. (Time required: 15-20 minutes)

1. Have the total assembly split into family groups, or small groups of 4-5 if families are not present.

2. Ask participants to think of the family in which they are now living. Present this situation: "Your family life has been quite busy. Three weeks ago the parent providing the main source of income had a heart attack. The doctor's report has just come in: complete rest and no more work for a year; thereafter, work may be possible but only on a part-time basis."

3. Have the groups talk about these questions:

   - Would some things change immediately for you personally? For the other family members? What immediate decisions would you need to make?

   - How would people outside your family unit be involved?

   - Would a typical day be different for you?

   - Are there things you would have to give up? What?

   - Would some things possibly change for the better? Why?

   - As you think about this situation, do you find any new insights or implications for your present family life?

Family Communications Questionnaire

Permission is given to reproduce this form for group and family use.

Our family communicates well together.
Our family does things together as a group.
Parent shows an interest in child's interests.
Child shows an interest in parent's interests.
Family members talk things over with each other.
Parent gives too much advice and lectures a lot.
Child respects parent's ideas and opinions.
Parent respects child's ideas and opinions.
Parent trusts child.
Child can discuss personal problems with parent.
Parent finds it hard to share feelings with family.
Child finds it hard to share feelings with parent.
Matters of sex are discussed.
Parent really listens to child.
Child really listens to parent.
Child hesitates to disagree with parent.
Parent explains reason for not letting child do something.
Parent tries to see child's side of things.
Child tries to see parent's side of things.
Parent shows confidence in child's abilities.

	Answered by PARENT			This column answered by YOUTH					
				My Mother			My Father		
	Yes	No	Pass	Yes	No	Pass	Yes	No	Pass

Family Communications Questionnaire

This exercise is for use with family groups who are willing to risk by going into considerable depth about how their own family members talk with and relate to one another.

The questionnaire is designed to help youth and their parents better understand how they communicate. Sharing perceptions and insights about family communications helps clear the air and can lead to deeper understanding and constructive action in family relationships. (Time required: 5 minutes to complete questionnaire and 15-20 minutes or more to share perceptions)

1. Duplicate the questionnaire and provide participants with a copy.

2. Have each family member complete the form in the appropriate columns, checking one of the three options (yes, no, pass). There are no right or wrong answers.

3. Have youth relate each item to their own personal experience in their family and have parents think of a specific child in their family, preferably one who will also fill out the questionnaire.

4. After participants have completed the form, invite parents and children to discuss the questionnaire content in any way they feel comfortable. Some family members may choose to compare their answers. Others may just want to discuss some issues raised. Participants who have no family members present can be combined into small groups for discussion. Some challenges to the small groups might be:

   • Share your perceptions in any way you feel comfortable.

   • Do you find one or two items your family can work on to improve communications? Decide who will do what to improve those communications.

   • Set a goal. (Pages 42-45 give purpose and procedure for Goal Setting.)

Generations Dialogue

This exercise works best if there are approximately equal numbers of youth and adults present. Its purpose is to create a setting for an intergenerational discussion, allowing youth and adults to share and learn from one another about important issues in family life. (Time required: at least 35-40 minutes)

1. Ask all youth to go to one side of the room, all adults to the other side.

2. Further divide the group into smaller units of 4 people, again keeping youth and adults separate. Note: Have the same number of subgroups on each side of the room (even if the number of persons in each subgroup is not the same).

3. Pass out a blank sheet of paper to each group and give the following instructions to everyone: "Shortly, I will be asking each of your groups to make a list of five things. You might think of more, but decide among yourselves on the top five. Appoint a recorder to write down the five things you decide on. Each group will need this list, because you will soon be breaking into new groups and sharing your list with some people on the other side of the room."

4. Give these instructions to the youth groups: "When you young people think about family life, what are some really important things (anything!) that you think adults should know about? Discuss these and put the five most important ones on your list."

   Give these instructions to the adult groups: "When you adults think about family life, what are some really important things (anything!) that you think young people should know about? Discuss these and put the five most important ones on your list.

5. Allow 15 minutes for groups to generate the list of items. Because groups work at different paces, slower ones may need to be pushed a bit. After 10 minutes, give a 5-minute warning. Call time and check to see that each group has a completed list.

6. Now pair each youth group with an adult group. Each group now has two lists.

7. Begin a sharing process. Have groups take the top item from one list, read it, and discuss it. They will then take the top item from the second list and repeat the process, taking alternate items until both lists have been shared and discussed. (Allow at least 15-20 minutes for this.) Check to see how the various groups are doing. Even though some groups will want more time, you may decide to call time while interest is still high. Or, if this is an ending exercise, groups can be allowed to finish at their own pace.

8. An optional way of concluding the exercise is to call everyone back together again to share their experiences and leanings with the total assembly.

Runaway

This exercise helps participants examine their thoughts, feelings, behaviors, and ways of communicating in a parent-child confrontation. (Time required: 15-20 minutes)

1. Read the following situation to the group:"Fourteen-year-old Connie and her parents have had quite a few disagreements recently about Connie's attitudes and behavior. She runs away from home and is gone three days and nights. The parents are desperate when they receive no word about her or from her. Late on the third day, Connie suddenly appears at the door."

2. Ask the group how they would probably react to this situation if they were Connie's parents.

3. On a chalkboard set up the columns and possible reactions as shown below.

4. Have the group rank their reactions in Column 1, from "most likely" to "least likely" (1 = most likely).

Column Column

1   2

____ ____ persuade her to see a counselor

____ ____ talk with her about what she has done

____ ____ accept and love her, no strings attached

____ ____ tell her she can't stay unless she promises to
change

____ ____ ground her for a certain length of time

____ ____ other:

5. Ask participants if they wish their ranking were different. I; so, have them do a ranking in Column 2 from
their "most preferred" action to their "least preferred."

6. Ask the total group to break into smaller groups of 3 or
4 and share:

- their rankings; what they would most likely do and
why.

- the changed rankings they would like to make.

- how their feelings and ranking would change if
Connie were a boy; if Connie were seventeen years
old instead of fourteen.

- whether Scripture gives any guidelines here.

7. Reassemble the total group and share comments and
learnings.

Family Strengths

This exercise may be completed together or individually. It helps family members become aware of their own
strengths and one another's strengths. (time required: 10-15
minutes)

1. Have participants make columns on a piece of paper.
Number of columns should equal the number of
people in their family. At the top of the columns, have
people write the names of family members, including
themselves.

2. Have participants look at one name at a time and think about that person.

   • What do you like about that person?

   • What strengths or good qualities does that person have? Have people write, in the columns, five strengths they see in each person listed. Caution participants to think only of strong points — nothing negative.

3. Ask participants to share their lists with their family. Offer these questions to think about:

   • What did you learn about your family while completing the exercise? About yourself?

   • What were your feelings about yourself and your family?

Marriage Poll

Polling gives participants an opportunity to state an important belief or idea and learn how others respond to it. Each person is also challenged to evaluate many other statements — a process which helps participants examine or reexamine their own attitudes, beliefs, and values regarding the marriage relationship. (Time required: 20 minutes plus discussion time)

1. Pass out one 4" x 6" card to each person.

2. Ask participants to think about the marriage relationship.

   • What makes it rich and rewarding?

   • Or, what makes it difficult?

3. Ask each person to write, at the top of the card, a short statement, summing up an important idea that he or she personally holds about marriage. The statement should be one that the individual believes strongly, can express in a sentence, and is willing to share.

4. Allow about 3 minutes for composing and writing the statements.

5. Ask participants to write the words *Agree, Strongly Agree, Disagree, Strongly Disagree,* and *Pass* in a column on the back of their cards.

6. Have participants spend about 10 minutes mining around the room, sharing their statement with each other and asking each person whether he or she agrees with the statement. Participants should get as many responses to their statements as they can, moving quickly from person to person and tabulating the responses on the back of the card. Caution participants not to discuss the issues. If need be, they should quickly clarify the statement to someone who doesn't understand it.

7. When time is up, reassemble the total group. Ask participants to determine what percent of the people agreed with their statements (number who agreed divided by total number of people who voted). Assure them that no value judgment is placed on the number who agree or disagree with their statement.

8. Ask for volunteers to read their statement and report on the number of persons who agreed with them.

9. Then ask the group to quickly call out words that describe underlying values about marriage which seem important to this group, identify areas of disagreement or conflict of values within the group, and call out any quotations from Scripture which they are reminded of.

10. Depending on time available, discussion may follow, either in the total group or in small groups.

Family Celebration

Christmas Gift-Giving

This exercise helps participants focus on giving and on the wide array of gifts associated with Christmas. It emphasizes the context in which gift-giving should take place for Christians. (Time required: 10- 15 minutes)

1. Reproduce the following page for each participant beforehand. Pass these out and allow 5-8 minutes of quiet time. Instruct persons to work alone, writing in responses to questions for each item.

2. After time is called, ask participants to think about these questions:

    • What kinds of feelings emerged as you completed this gift-giving exercise?

    • Which gifts were most difficult for you to identify?

3. Ask participants to share their thoughts and feelings with one other person.

What two talents would you like to share with others?

What Christmas message about the Christian faith would you give to all?

What gift would you like to give to your family?

What gift that you gave another was especially liked?

What would you give to Jesus Christ?

What gift could you give to the Church?

What is the best gift you ever got?

What Christmas gift you received has special memories?

What is a gift you created?

Celebration

1. Have each family member list ten things they love to do at Christmas.

2. After participants have completed their lists, give these instructions:

   - Star your top four.
   - Put a dollar sign by those that cost money.
   - Put an **F** by those you do as a family.
   - Put an **A** by those you prefer to do alone.
   - Put an **O** by those that involve doing something for other people.
   - Put a **T** by those that involve a tradition in your family.
   - Put a **C** by those that involve church.
   - Put a **W** by those you wish you would do with your family.

3. Have participants study their coded lists for a few minutes. Ask if they see any patterns regarding the things they love? Allow time to share any discoveries.

4. For family discussion:

   - Compare your top four with others in your family.
   - Can you come to a consensus on what is your favorite thing to do at Christmas as a family?
   - How many preferences do you share with the other members of your family?
   - What is one thing you would like to see become a part of your family's celebration at Christmas? Why is it important to you?
   - Are there some things you would like to change in your Christmas celebration? Which?
   - Action: If there are some new things you would like to introduce, or some changes you would like to make, why not try them?

Three Levels of Learning

This exercise provides an opportunity for parents and/or youth to examine parent-child relationships, focusing on the importance of keeping the relationship intact despite differences.

Give Me the Facts!
(See Luke 24:41-52)
Questions to answer:

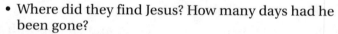

- When did Jesus and his family go to Jerusalem?

- What concern did Mary and Joseph have as they started back home?

- Where did they find Jesus? How many days had he been gone?

- What was he doing?

- What did Mary say to him?

- How did Jesus answer?

What's the Idea?
Concepts to explore:

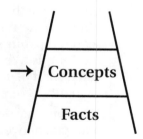

- Why was the Feast of the Passover celebrated every year? Find out all you can about it.

- What time in the life of a Christian youth parallels this time when Jesus went to the Temple?

- What kind of feelings did Jesus probably have for the Temple?

- What kind of understanding do you think Mary had for Jesus' deep interest in the Temple?

What's in It for Me?

Valuing suggestions: (Time required: at least *20-30* minutes)

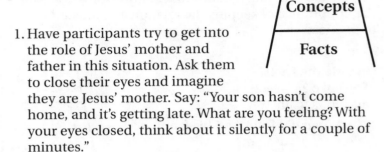

1. Have participants try to get into the role of Jesus' mother and father in this situation. Ask them to close their eyes and imagine they are Jesus' mother. Say: "Your son hasn't come home, and it's getting late. What are you feeling? With your eyes closed, think about it silently for a couple of minutes."

2. Now ask them to imagine they are Jesus' father, wondering where their son is. Say: "What are you feeling? What are you saying to your spouse at this frantic moment? Think about it for a minute or so."

3. Have participants open their eyes and pair up with a person alongside them. Have the pairs spend 2-3 minutes sharing the thoughts and feelings they had as Jesus' parent.

4. Have each pair quickly designate a parent and a son in their pair and close their eyes again. Say: "Sons, imagine you have spent three busy days learning from others in the Temple. Parents, imagine you go on a search for your son. After three days you find him in the Temple. What is the first thing you do when you catch sight of each other? (Pause.) What do you say to each other?"

5. Now have participants open their eyes and try a brief dialogue between parent and son. Say: "Parents, express your thoughts and feelings to your son in any manner you feel appropriate at this moment. Say the words — along with any gestures and feelings. Sons, how do you view the situation? What are your thoughts and feelings? Try expressing them to your parent. You may begin."

6. After a 2-3 minute dialogue, stop the pairs and have them take a couple of minutes to talk with each other about the dialogue they shared. Ask: "What are your thoughts and feelings about it?" Have them share their reactions or insights.

7. Have each pair combine with another pair into groups of 4 to talk about the experience. They may want to consider one or more of these questions:

    • Do you think Jesus' parents saw him as rebelling?

    • Does this situation relate to your own family experience? How?

    • Adults, are there times when you thought a child was rebelling, and he or she was only doing something in a different way?

    • Young people, was there a time when you felt misunderstood because you were doing something different from what was expected?

8. After terminating the small group exercise, form two larger groups — an adult group and a youth group. Have the two groups meet separately to do some quick brainstorming. Instruct the groups to brainstorm some differences of opinion which tend to separate the generations. (Caution the groups not to discuss or judge the items — just list as many as they can think of.)

9. Have the groups compare their lists.

    • Were there any similar discoveries? What were they?

10. Have groups agree on a topic that needs particular clarification or better communication.

11. Plan another session on that topic, using a Listening exercise, Interview, etc.

Resources from the Bible
(for optional use)

Marriage

Ephesians 5:21	Be subject to one another out of reverence for Christ.
Galatians 3:28	Neither male nor female; all one in Jesus Christ.
Genesis 2:18	Companionship.
Genesis 2:24	One flesh.
Matthew 19:3-9	Christ confirms the Old Testament creation pattern of marriage.
Malachi 2:14-16	Faithfulness.
Ephesians 5:33	Love and respect.
Proverbs 31:10-31	A good wife — who can find?
1 John 4:7	Loving one another.
Matthew 19:3-12 and Mark 10:2-12	Jesus appealed to Genesis 1:27 and 2:24 for his basic argument.
Ruth 1:16	Wherever you go.

Women

John 4:1-42	Jesus talked with women frequently, announced his messiahship to a Samaritan woman.
Luke 10:38-42	Jesus talked with women about religion.
Gospel of Luke	Much about women.
John 20:11	Women bear witness of the risen Jesus.
Matthew 28:9 Mark 16:9	

Women and the Church
1 Corinthians 11:7-16
1 Corinthians 14:26-35
1 Timothy 2:9-14

Children and Parents

Ephesians 6:14	Do not provoke your children to anger.
Colossians 3:20	Obedience to parents.
Colossians 3:21	Do not provoke your children, lest they become discouraged.
Deuteronomy 6:4-7	Teaching in family.
1 Timothy 5:34	Children's duty to family.
Ephesians 4:12-16; Colossians 3:12-25; Romans 12; 1 Corinthians 13	Building each other up in love for a Gospel-oriented family.
Proverbs 22:6	Child-raising.

New Life in Christ
Colossians 1:9-14; 2:1-23; 3:1-25 through 4:1
2 Corinthians 5:17

New Commandment
Matthew 22:37-39

A New Way of Love
1 Corinthians 13:8-13
Ephesians 4:13-16
1 John 3:1-14

Prayer

Lord, thank you for the family. What a beautiful creation! We have sometimes distorted and lost sight of what you meant it to be. Forgive us!

I want to be a loving family member — a listener, an encourager, and a support to those around me. I know that the kind of love a family desperately needs is the love that you introduced — a patient, giving kind of love.

Give each one of us a rich measure of that love so that we will grow into a healthy, whole, and caring family.

Valuing Myself and My Gifts

We believe that each person is a special gift of God and that each person has God given talents that can be shared with others. But many personal strengths and gifts go undiscovered throughout a person's life. Or they often get lost in a climate which tends to emphasize the negative rather than the positive.

We believe that people need to take time to identify their talents and strengths; but being aware of them is not enough. We need to ask ourselves: Are we using these gifts in our day-to-day living not only to please ourselves but also to please others and God?

When we know who we are and to whom we belong, we are more free to use our talents and to celebrate them. Through greater awareness, caring, and sharing, we become whole persons who feel better about ourselves as creatures of God.

Before using this chapter, please review the chapter on leadership.

 ## Voting

Instructions: Pages 30-31 give purpose and procedure for the Voting exercise.

Participants vote in the following manner:

Agree?	(Raise hand.)
Strongly agree?	(Wave hand.)
Disagree?	(Thumb down.)
Strongly disagree?	(Shake thumb.)
Pass?	(Fold arms across chest.)

General Voting Questions

How many of you:

- think that the real meaning of life can be found mainly through service to others?
- think that, should you die today, your life has been worthwhile?
- think that your faith makes a difference in your outlook on life?
- feel O.K. about not going along with the crowd?
- are sometimes concerned about what others think?
- like to try new things?
- measure success by your own standards, rather than by others' standards?
- would like to offer your talents to the Church but don't know how to go about it?
- are satisfied with how you spend your time?
- think that giving always means sacrifice?
- think that most people feel guilty when they are not doing something "productive?"
- find it hard to discipline your use of time?
- often find that what you actually do contradicts what you say you believe?
- think sacrificial giving should be a condition of church membership?
- stop and think occasionally about the worth of what you're doing?
- take time to think about what you value in life?
- have nearly the same values you had five years ago?
- are often torn between what you want to do and what you believe is right?
- feel that your values form a real basis for your decisions and actions?
- think that values come naturally to a person, with no need to "work" at them?
- think certain things we value actually become false gods?

My Outlook on Life
How many of you:

- think that life is brimming over with exciting, good things?
- think that most people spend more time thinking about themselves than about others?
- think that to admire ourselves as we are makes us too complacent?
- think that most people have trouble dealing with their real feelings?
- think that most people have negative feelings about themselves?
- think that people who expect the worst in life usually find it?
- think that some are lucky in life and some are not?
- think that most people value good looks more than inner beauty?
- think that a person's ideas and beliefs are greatly influenced by how much money he or she has?
- think that people are basically good and have great potential to love and care?
- think that people have a natural desire to grow and learn?

My View of Myself
How many of you:

- understand yourself pretty well?
- are often a puzzle to yourself?
- would like to understand yourself better?
- think that God has something to do with who you are right now?
- depend on God for direction?
- think that you have to step on someone to get ahead?
- did something this week that you are proud of?

Roland S. Larson & Doris E. Larson   151

- are bored by routine?
- feel on top of the world when you reach a goal you set?
- think you learn more when you go through the struggles of making your own choices?
- think that talking over the consequences of your choice helps clarify your thoughts?
- gave up a hobby because you weren't good at it?
- are perfectionists?

My View of Myself and Others
How many of you:

- are happy with your life-style?
- have experienced feelings of loneliness?
- believe that good can come from your struggles?
- are greatly influenced by your family?
- are easily swayed by your friends?
- wish people really knew you as you are?
- feel that people appreciate you for who you are?
- worry a lot?
- usually want to please others?
- usually work too hard at pleasing yourself?
- did not share a new idea with someone because you were afraid the person might laugh at you?
- would be willing to take a cut in salary as part of a long-range effort to improve living conditions for others?
- love others as much as you love yourself?

Things I Like
How many of you:

- like to be around people?
- like to daydream?
- would like to fly an airplane?

- enjoy skiing?
- like to meditate?
- would like to meet a well-known leader?
- would like to be a famous leader?
- like to sleep late in the morning?
- like to be around older people?
- would like to be rich?
- like birthday parties?
- enjoy making things?
- like to play with young children?
- make music an important part of your life?

Loving My Neighbor and Myself
How many of you agree with this statement?

- Showing love is hard to do.
- Loving oneself is difficult.
- Loving oneself is healthy.
- "Keeping up with the Joneses" is a way for some people to feel O.K.
- Being "successful" doesn't prove we're good persons.
- Being self-critical is necessary for growth.
- We are all worthwhile human beings. We begin to love ourselves when we stop condemning and accusing ourselves.
- How a person acts is determined more by other people than by oneself.
- It is easy to be yourself.
- God accepts you as you are.
- God wants you to be different than you are now.
- God has a special mission for you.
- People usually act first and then find reasons to explain their behavior.

Success
How many of you:

- feel successful?
- think that success takes hard work?
- think that a successful person is usually wealthy?
- think that success is the feeling that you are doing your best?
- have changed your ideas of what success means during the last five years?
- think that for many people, success refers only to material things?
- have ever felt successful, yet found that no one recognized your success?
- think that Jesus was successful?
- think that success is liking yourself?
- think that success is knowing and standing up for what you believe?
- think that success is a goal to be reached by age 50 or 60?
- think that success is the capacity to change?
- think that success is allowing yourself to become the person God intends?
- think that success is living responsibly in society?
- think that ambition makes people do inhuman things?
- think that the amount of money a person makes depends on how hard that person works?
- think jobs with power and prestige mean increased satisfaction and happiness?
- get most of your satisfaction in life from your job?
- would like to retire early?
- think that people who work only for their own glory seldom find real joy in their work?

My Gifts

How many of you agree with this statement?

- Musical ability is a gift.
- Leadership ability is a gift.
- A warm smile is a gift.
- You are a capable person.
- You have many strengths.
- You have a unique contribution to make to the world.
- Talking about personal strengths is embarrassing.
- Talking about personal strengths is boastful.
- A person can have a Christian vocation outside the Church.
- It is difficult to be open and honest with other church members about one's personal concerns.
- People need the Church as a support when they have problems.
- The Church is accepting of people as they are.
- Some people participate in a church activity because they feel it is their duty.
- Using our gifts to serve others is one way of thanking God.

Management of Time

How many of you:

- can usually account for your time?
- think you usually manage your time wisely?
- clutter your days with trivia?
- often set daily goals?
- try to set aside time for meditation and devotions each day?
- often put off doing distasteful tasks?
- wish you could organize your time better?
- consider time as a gift from God?

- think it's better to take each day as it comes rather than planning far ahead?
- feel O.K. about taking time to "goof off?"
- think you waste a lot of time watching TV?
- think mostly about the past?
- think more about the future than the past?
- think that one can spend too much time with community or church activities at the expense of one's personal life?

Gifts of Money

How many of you agree with this statement?

- People should give first and think about it later.
- People *think* about giving more than they actually give.
- The things people spend money on tell a lot about the quality of their faith.
- Those who give generously to the Church are usually blessed materially in return.
- The tithe (10% of income) is a good standard to use in giving to the Church.
- Church members should be allowed to designate the use of their tithe.
- To be both rich and Christian is not possible. If we are Christians, we are not free to spend our money as we wish.
- People should use any extra money to help others.
- The more you have, the more you should give to others. Money is the root of all evil. Money is a gift from God.
- The Lord will provide, so we don't need to.
- There is nothing wrong with money if it's used for a good cause.

Leisure

How many of you:

- set aside a special time each week for leisure activities you enjoy?
- think everyone needs free time?
- think that Christians should observe the Sabbath by resting from work?
- think that Americans are too driven by the "work ethic?"
- would like a four-day work week?
- would take a salary cut for a shorter work week?
- feel that leisure time is a luxury for the rich?
- think that one needs to discipline the use of free time?
- would rather spend most of your leisure time by yourself than with others?
- feel that having a hobby or a special interest would encourage you to use more leisure time?
- feel that leisure time implies neglect in other areas?

Work

How many of you:

- like your job?
- work long hours?
- are hooked on work?
- get more enjoyment from your leisure hours than you get on the job?
- find your work interfering with your personal life?
- are sometimes frustrated with too much free time?

Ranking

Instructions: Pages 31-32 give purpose and procedure for the Ranking exercise.

Participants rank all items in order of preference or priority (1 = most important; 2 = next most important, etc.).

Outlook on Life
Which is most important to you?

____ living responsibly

____ being insightful

____ being well liked

____ being physically attractive

Which gives you the most satisfaction?

____ high marks

____ learning something new

____ solving a problem

Which is most important to you?

____ new adventures

____ service to others

____ good personal relationships

What is most important to you in life?

____ to be a good spouse

____ to be a good parent

____ to be a whole person

____ to be a good friend

____ to be a good daughter or son

What is most important to you?

____ to do well in a chosen job

____ to have a good social life

____ to feel good about yourself

Which is most important to you?

____ status

____ money

____ comfort

View of Self

How do you see yourself?

____ as a decision maker

____ as a peacemaker

____ as an innovator

Which most nearly describes you?

____ critical

____ easygoing

____ demanding of others

From which do your talents stem?

____ hands

____ head

____ heart

How do you feel you are using your talents?

____ very well

____ pretty well

____ not so well

How do you see yourself?

____ I am attractive to others.

____ I'm not too popular.

____ I get along with others.

Compared to most others, which describes you?

____ more intelligent

____ less intelligent

____ just as intelligent

Which is most important in your life?

____ feeling good about yourself

____ a family that loves you

____ good friends to relate to

____ financial security

Which would you rather risk?

____ the effects of permanent unemployment

____ the effects of lung cancer

____ the effects of an earthquake

Which quality do you most prefer in others?

____ friendliness

____ honesty

____ unselfishness

Which would you rather be?

____ a well-liked boss

____ a respected politician

____ a famous artist

Which would you rather be?

____ a farmer

____ a business person

____ a youth corrections worker

What trait would you prefer in a friend of the opposite sex?

____ creativity

____ humor

____ attractiveness

With which church group would you rather work?

____ youth group

____ council/board

____ church-school children

How would you rather spend a free afternoon?

____ alone outdoors

____ puttering around the house

____ socializing with friends

How do you rank the following statements?

____ Playing and relaxing is as important as hard work.

____ Free time should be used to help others.

____ Hard work is a virtue; time not spent on work is time wasted.

Gifts to the Church
Which church activities would enable you to become more
aware of your personal strengths or your personal gifts?
(Rank each group of three separately.)

____ attending church worship

____ attending confirmation class

____ attending church summer camp

____ visiting a nursing home

____ helping on a church-sponsored car wash

____ being an usher

____ helping serve Communion -teaching church school
        singing in the choir

____ serving on the church council

____ working on a stewardship drive

____ becoming a priest or minister

What keeps you from sharing more of your money?

____ material needs and desires

____ saving for the future

____ supporting family members

How much money should people give to the Church?

____ all they can spare

____ a tenth of their gross income

____ no set amount

Success
Which is success most like?

____ winning

____ feeling you've done your best

____ accomplishing something

What is most important to you in choosing a career?

_____ prestige

_____ money

_____ service

_____ personal fulfillment

Continuum

Instructions: Pages 32-33 give purpose and procedure for the Continuum exercise.

Participants choose that place on the continuum, between two opposite extremes, which most closely represents their personal viewpoint.

Work and Leisure Time

How do you prefer to spend your time?

|——————————————————————————|

alone   with people

How much do you use your talents?

|——————————————————————————|

never   always

Given the opportunity would you work more, or less?

|——————————————————————————|

much more   much less

How do you spend your leisure time?

|——————————————————————————|

pleasing myself   serving others

How much time do you spend watching television?

|——————————————————————————|

never turn it off   never turn it on

What does Sunday mean to you?

|—————————————————————————————|

It's a special day to be   It's the same as any
observed by worship and rest.   other day.

View of Self
To what extent should a person express feelings to others?

|—————————————————————————————|

Be open; express all   Keep feelings to oneself.
feelings.

Which describes you most of the time?

|—————————————————————————————|

pessimistic   optimistic

How should a person deal with anger?

|—————————————————————————————|

Express it freely.   Hold it in.

Which best describes you?

|—————————————————————————————|

I always lead.   I always follow.

How do you deal with conflict?

|—————————————————————————————|

Avoid conflict at all costs.   Confront — bring conflict
into open.

Which are you more like?

|—————————————————————————————|

private   social

Success
How do you feel about competition?

|—————————————————————————————|

Win at all costs.   Winning is unimportant.

When you accomplish something what do you do?

|———————————————————————————|

Tell everyone about it.　　　　　　　　Tell no one about it.

Giving

Do you feel that you have talents to share?

|———————————————————————————|

none at all　　　　　　　　　　　　　　　many

Do you enjoy sharing the talents you have?

|———————————————————————————|

not much　　　　　　　　　　　　　　very much

Are you a spender or a saver?

|———————————————————————————|

spender　　　　　　　　　　　　　　　　saver

Either/Or

Instructions: Pages 34-35 give purpose and procedure for the Either/Or exercise.

Participants select between two choices that option with which they most closely identify.

View of Self

Which are you more like:
     giving / taking
     arguing / agreeing
     helping watching
     active / passive
     willow / oak
     cello / trumpet
     competitive / cooperative
     taking off / digging in
     problem solver / worrier

Which is more important to you?
> personal freedom / following the rules
> a lucrative job / a meaningful job
> adventure / recognition

In the biblical story of Mary and Martha (Luke 10:38-42) which are you more like?
> Mary / Martha

Success
Which are you most apt to admire?
> leader / poet
> entertainer / teacher
> scientist / artist
> athlete / doctor
> courage / generosity
> wisdom / honor
> ability / good will

Giving
Which is more important to the Church?
> how much I give / how much I do

Which do you spend more on?
> wants / needs self / others

To which would you most likely give?
> medical research / recreation facilities
> save our schools / save our parks
> chemical dependency program / day-care center
> political candidate / guest-lecture program
> congregational needs / world relief

Listening

Instructions: Pages 35-37 give purpose and procedure for the Listening exercise.

Participants respond to a stimulus statement in groups of three. Each person is "on focus" for five minutes.

General Listening Statements

Jack complained: "There's just too much disagreement among Christians about what's right and what's wrong. The reason, I think, is that sometimes the Bible itself isn't very clear. Like, is killing or stealing always wrong? Most Christians don't seem to know for sure, so they end up doing whatever they want."

Spence said, "A friend of mine is the most thankful person I've ever met. I don't know how he does it, but he's able to thank God for everything, good or bad. He can actually offer thanks to God when something destructive or negative happens to him. Personally, I can't thank God for the suffering that happens to another person. I can't thank God for hunger and oppression in the world. I think that's going a bit too far — thanking God for those kinds of things."

Work and Leisure

Jan said, "Time is a gift from God. We should make the best use of every moment, every day. A person should decide what's important to do today and let nothing interfere. God is going to ask us to account for every minute we waste."

Ron wanted the fellows to know how he felt so he said, "A Christian is a person who knows how to work, how to give 110 percent in everything he or she does. God intended people to work and work hard. This is how we can fulfill our fives and further the Kingdom of God."

Giving

Norma said, "Every Christian should be a servant. It's more important to put the needs of other persons before your own, even if you have to suffer. We need to forget about ourselves and serve God by helping others. This is what Jesus meant when he said, 'Anyone who wants to become great among you must be slave to all.'

Mark listened intently as Richard said, "You might think I'm un-Christian, but frankly I think money is one of the most important things in life. It's true that Jesus warned against the dangers of riches, but he also praised the unjust steward for being prudent. When I was young our family was really poor, and I can tell you that poverty didn't bring us closer to God. God expects us to use common sense — to take care of our families now and to provide for a decent old age."

Kate said, "The early Christians owned everything in common. A life-style like that would be good for our society. We could ease poverty if we shared more of our wealth. And think what we could do for ecology by sharing cars, land, and appliances. We would also discover how important we are to each other. Most Americans don't realize that."

Dilemma

Instructions: Pages 37-39 give purpose and procedure for the Dilemma exercise.

Participants respond to a dilemma situation, exploring alternatives and consequences and finally choosing their own best solution.

Sharing Gifts

Your spouse confides to you: "I don't know why, but our neighbor has offered to teach Sunday school. She doesn't seem to like kids much and yells at them when they com into her yard. She knows we're short of teachers and wants to help, but our son will be in her class and he's frightened of her. What can we do?" What do you say?

You are the church choir director. One day a member of the congregation stops you and says: "I'd like to sing in the choir, but I don't have much of a voice, and I can't read music. I suppose I ought to confine my singing to the shower." What do you say?

Your church is sponsoring a drive for a cause you do not believe in. One of your neighbors is heading the drive and has asked you to contribute. What do you do?

Interviewing

Instructions: Pages 39-43 give purpose and procedure for the Interviewing exercise.

A volunteer from among the participants is interviewed before the group.

Select appropriate questions from pages 40-41. In addition you might want to consider these questions:

- What do you like to do when you are alone?
- How important are people in your life?
- What special skills do you have?
- What major influences have made you the person you are today?
- What does the word *success* mean to you?
- Have your ideas about success changed over the years?
- Was there a time you felt particularly successful?
- En what area do you feel most successful now?
- What news items most disturb you these days?
- Is there one thing you would like to do or accomplish before you die?
- What will you probably be doing five or ten years from now? What would you like to be doing then?

Miscellaneous Exercises

The remaining exercises in this section are one of a kind. The purpose of each is to help participants further examine what they believe and value about themselves and their gifts. Procedures are given for each.

Modern Exodus

This exercise helps participants think about their most meaningful possessions and prioritize them. (Time required: 10-15 minutes)

1. Give these instructions: "A catastrophe is upon your city, and you must leave your home without ever returning to claim your possessions. You are allowed to take a maximum of eight items with you. You must be able to carry them to an evacuation station about four blocks away. Quickly list the eight items. Do not include other people. They are taken care of." (Allow about 3 minutes.)

2. After participants have completed their lists, have them gather in groups of 4 and share:

   - the three or four most important items you saved.

   - why they are important to you.

   - what you thought of as you made your choices.

   - what you learned about yourself from the choices you made.

Self-Evaluation I

1. Reproduce the Self-Evaluation form which follows andpass out a copy to each participant.

2. Have participants read the instructions and complete the form independently.

3. When the forms have been completed, ask participants if they would prefer to be at different places on any of the continuums. If so, suggest that they might wish to set a goal to accomplish that. (Pages 42-45 give purpose and procedure for Goal Setting.)

Self-Evaluation Form

Instructions: On each continuum below, underline the number that best represents where you are now and circle the number that best represents where you'd like to be.

Living up to my beliefs:

1	2	3	4	5	6	7	8	9	10

Never   Always

Attending church:

1	2	3	4	5	6	7	8	9	10

Never   Always

Giving according to my ability:

1	2	3	4	5	6	7	8	9	10

Never   Always

Sharing myself with others:

1	2	3	4	5	6	7	8	9	10

Never   Always

Listening to members of my family:

1	2	3	4	5	6	7	8	9	10

Never   Always

Spending time with people I love:

1	2	3	4	5	6	7	8	9	10

Never   Always

Spending time alone with God:

1	2	3	4	5	6	7	8	9	10

Never   Always

Using my talents:

1	2	3	4	5	6	7	8	9	10

Never   Always

Permission is given to reproduce this page for family and group use.

Self-Evaluation II

1. Have participants compile the following lists:
   - three things you like to do on a rainy day
   - three books you have read and enjoyed
   - three things you like best about yourself
   - three new and good things in your life
   - three things you can do well
   - three concerns you have

2. Ask volunteers to share one thing they learned about themselves from completing their lists.

Motivations for Attending Church

This exercise helps participants examine and discuss some reasons why people attend church and also gives them insights into their own motivations. (Time required: about 30 minutes, depending on group size)

1. Have the group form two circles, one inside the other, facing each other. Have each participant in the outer circle pair with a participant in the inner circle. Explain that the group will be exploring some possible motivations for attending church.

2. From the list given below, read the first possible motivation for attending church. You might say: "People attend church for various reasons. One reason may be social: to meet people and be with friends."

3. Ask each pair to react to the social motivation by discussing these questions:
   - What do you think of this as a reason for attending church?
   - Do you, personally, ever attend church for this reason? (Allow 2-3 minutes for pairs to discuss these two questions.)

4. After the pairs have completed their discussion, give these instructions: "We are now ready to consider the next motivation, but first we will change partners. People in the inside circle stay seated. Persons in the outside circle move one seat to the left."

5. Give the new partners another motivation from the list below, and have them follow the same procedure.

6. Repeat, until participants have considered 6-8 reasons, or until everyone has talked with every possible partner.

Motivations for attending church:

- To meet people and be with friends.
- To grow in faith.
- Out of a sense of duty.
- To make business contacts.
- To appear respectable.
- To get out of the house.
- To hear a good sermon.
- To satisfy conscience.
- Because friends belong.
- To set an example.
- To be intellectually challenged.
- To find a mate, a girlfriend or boyfriend.
- As an excuse to dress up for a change.
- To help fulfill a commitment to Jesus Christ.
- (Any others participants wish to add.)

7. Reassemble the group. Invite volunteers to share insights, reactions.

Work Motivations

This exercise gives an opportunity to examine some motivations for pursuing a career. (Time required: 20-30 minutes or more, depending on group size)

Pages 173-174 (Motivations for Attending Church) give the procedure for this exercise.

Possible motivations for working:

- To further personal and family interests; to support a family.
- To develop and use personal talents.
- To help other people; to make the world a better place to live.
- To be challenged and stimulated.
- To further the work of God on earth.
- To have money for a few luxuries.
- To keep from being bored or feeling useless.
- (Any others participants wish to add.)

Success Motivations

This exercise helps participants examine some of their thoughts, feelings, and drives related to success. (Time required: 20-30 minutes, depending on group size)

Pages 173-174 (Motivations for Attending Church) give the procedure for this exercise.

Possible motivations for wanting to be "successful":

- To have more material things.
- To gain the respect of others.
- To keep up with others.
- To demonstrate self-achievement.
- To please parents or other people.
- For personal security.
- For influence and power.
- (Any others participants wish to add.)

My Gifts

This exercise helps people recognize and value the gifts God has given them. (Time required: 25-30 minutes or more)

1. Hand out blank sheets of paper, and have each participant number down the page from one to ten.

2. Ask them to list the gifts they have — the things they do well.

3. Have participants look over their lists and place a star beside the gifts they really enjoy using.

4. Have participants gather in groups of 4 to share their lists. Ask that they focus on one person at a time, helping that person identify the gifts and abilities he or she might have missed.

5. Ask the group to spend a moment or two considering their abilities and how they might use them to help others.

6. Have each group of 4 divide into pairs. Ask that each person choose one or two of their gifts and help one another think of ways these gifts can be of value to others. Questions to discuss:

   • How can these gifts be used to help another person or a community of people?

   • Can they be used in your church?

7. Invite participants to set a goal. (Pages 42-45 give the procedure for Goal Setting.)

8. Reassemble the total group, and give these suggestions:

   • Think about the list you made. Was it difficult to identify your gifts? Were you surprised to discover you could list so many? Or so few?

   • Can a few of you tell what you learned or share an insight you gained? Try completing this sentence, "I learned that.

Windfall
(Time required: 15-20 minutes)

1. Present this situation to the total group:

   "Your wealthy uncle, who was a great philanthropist, just died and left you a large sum of money. After taxes and other costs, you have $160,000.

   "The will stipulates that you must give away at least half of your inheritance within the next two years. The money must be given 'to further the growth of Christianity in individual lives, in any manner that seems effective to you.'

   "The terms are open. Apparently your uncle knew you well enough to trust your judgment.

   "Without worrying about legal procedures or other details, and working alone, consider where and how you will allocate the $80,000."

2. After about 5 minutes, have participants gather in groups of 4 to share choices and discuss the values that underlie those choices.

Relationships

This exercise gives people an opportunity to examine the influence of relationships on their lives. (Time required: about 15 minutes)

1. Ask each participant to draw a line down the middle of a piece of paper. In one column, have them list people who have been important in their lives. In the other column, have them list why the person has been important.

2. When participants have completed their lists, have the group pair off. In pairs, participants take turns talking about their lists with one another. Have them see if they find any common elements that tell something about their meaningful relationships with others.

3. Invite volunteers from the total group to complete this statement: "My most meaningful relationships seem to be, . . ."

The Gift of Leadership

Throughout history we find a wide variety of leadership styles. Effective leadership takes many forms — often reflecting the personality, background, and past experiences of the leader. This exercise provides participants with the opportunity to reflect on styles of leadership, including their own. (Time required: 15-20 minutes)

1. Have each participant think about committees on which they have served in the community, church, or school. Have them try to recall various styles of leadership from their experiences. Then ask participants to rank, from most effective (1) to least effective (4), the examples given below. You may wish to write these descriptions on the chalkboard:

   Person A: Keeps things moving; influences group decisions subtly and tactfully.

   Person B: Participates as member of group; seeks others' contributions; guides group to its own decisions.

   Person C. Asserts self in strong and direct manner; efficient; gets results.

   Person D: Keeps peace at all costs; avoids conflict; often assumes major responsibility to get the job done.

2. When the group has completed their rankings, have them gather in groups of 4 to share their rankings. (Allow 2-3 minutes.)

3. Ask each group if it can agree on some important principles for effective leadership. (Allow 2-3 minutes.)

4. Ask participants to think about the following individually:

   • Which of the four styles most nearly reflects your own personal way of leading?

- Are you satisfied with that?
- Are there changes you would like to try which might increase your effectiveness in leadership?

5. Have participants find a partner and share some thoughts about their own style of leadership. Ask that they try to be helpful to one another — listening and giving feedback. (Allow 5-10 minutes.)

Portrait

This exercise gives people an opportunity to become more visually aware of others and more aware of themselves by using feedback from others' impressions of them. (Time required: 10-15 minutes)

1. Ask participants to find a partner. Give these instructions:

"Sit facing your partner. In each pair designate Person A and Person B.

"Imagine that each of you is a portrait painter; you will have a chance to paint a mental portrait of your partner.

"Without talking, look at your partner and observe his or her features — eyes, hair, coloring, expression — for about 30-40 seconds. (Pause.)

"Now close your eyes. Person A, describe to Person B the portrait you are mentally painting of him or her."

2. After a few minutes, have partners reverse roles. Person B describes Person A.

3. Ask pairs to share:
- what you learned about yourself.
- what you learned about each other.
- what you see as important in your own physical appearance.
- what you see as important in the other's appearance.

Memories

(Time required: 10-15 minutes)

Jesus said: .. . . unless you change and become like little
children you will never enter the kingdom of heaven.
And so, the one who makes himself as little as this
little child is the greatest in the kingdom of heaven."
(Matthew 18:3-4)

1. Have each participant think of himself or herself as a
small child; or have them think of a small child they
have recently observed. Ask: "What qualities or characteristics attract you? Make a list of these characteristics." (Allow 5 minutes.)

2. Have participants share the following in pairs:

   • Which of the qualities you listed do you have now?

   • Have some that you had as a small child been lost
   along the way? Which?

   • Are there one or two you would really like to have
   again? If so, discuss ways you can recapture these.
   (Allow 5 minutes.)

3. Invite participants to set a personal goal. (Pages 42-45
give procedure for Goal Setting.)

Birthday Celebration

Celebrating My Strengths

This exercise invites participants to identify and
celebrate their successes, strengths, and values.

1. Duplicate the form "Celebrating My Strengths" and
provide a copy for each participant.

2. Have participants think about their most recent
birthday. Suggest that they probably accomplished
many things over the years and that some of these
may have gone unrecognized. Explain to participants
that they will be doing a birthday inventory to give
their accomplishments and strengths recognition.

3. Have participants list as many of their accomplishments as they can think of in the "success" candle, using words or short phrases to describe them. (Allow about 5 minutes.)

4. Have each participant find a partner, preferably someone he or she knows quite well. Have partners share their accomplishments with each other. Give these instructions: "As you look over your list, what strengths do you find in yourself? With your partner, identify your personal strengths and list them in the "strengths" candle. (Allow about 10 minutes.)

5. Now have participants work alone for a few minutes, adding other strengths — ones that were not identified with their partners. Encourage them to list as many positive qualities as they can think of. (Allow another 2-3 minutes.)

6. Give these instructions: "As you think about your accomplishments and your strengths, what do they suggest to you about the values you hold? List the five values that seem most important to you. Write them in the "values" candle. (Allow 5 minutes.)

7. Continue: "Look at your list of strengths and your list of important values. If you apply your strengths to the things that are important to you, what is one new success you could make happen? With your partner, set a goal to make this success happen. Tell your partner what you will do, how you will do it, and when." (Pages 42-45 give procedure for Goal Setting. Allow 10-15 minutes.)

8. Have partners combine with another pair to share some of their discoveries.

9. Invite the group to think of a special way to celebrate their personal successes and strengths.

Celebrating My Strengths

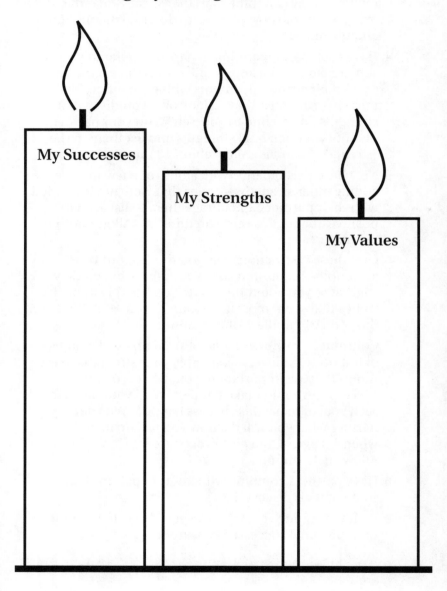

My Successes

My Strengths

My Values

Permission is given to reproduce this page for family and group use.

Three Levels of Learning

Give Me the Facts!
(See Matthew 25:14-30, the Parable of the Talents)
Questions to answer:

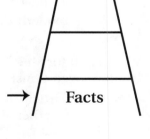

- What is a talent? (Check in a Bible dictionary or encyclopedia.)
- How did the man divide his property?
- Why were different amounts given to each servant?
- How did the first two servants account for their stewardship when the master returned?
- What did the master say to these two servants when he learned how each had used the talents?
- How did the servant with the one talent use his? What reason did he give?
- How did the master respond to him?
- What did Jesus say that summed up the meaning of this parable?

What's the Idea?
Concepts to explore:

- What does this parable tell us about the way God views our gifts?
- How might the master have responded if the servant with one talent had risked in a business venture and lost some or all of it?
- How might this statement be explained: "Every Christian is a steward of the gospel."
- What are some obstacles to Christian stewardship?

- What excuses might be offered to avoid stewardship responsibilities?

- To what extent are people in the Church today guilty of hoarding their gifts?

- What modern-day title could be given to this parable?

What's in It for Me?
Valuing suggestions:

1. Have participants take time to reflect on their lives and then list their talents.

2. Ask participants to imagine themselves in a parable similar to the Parable of the Talents in which they must account for their use of talents. Ask if anything keeps them from using their talents?

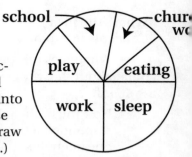

Values

Concepts

Facts

3. Have participants consider their use of time as well as talents. Ask:

   - How long have you lived?

   - Can you describe how you have used that time?

   - How do you hope to use your time in the future?

4. When participants have had a chance to consider the preceding questions, give these instructions: "Think about your typical day. Draw a circle and divide it into segments that show how you use your day." (You might wish to draw this example on the chalkboard.)

   Allow about 5 minutes, then continue: "Now draw another circle and divide it into time- segments that show how you *wish* you would spend your day."

5. Have participants share their drawings in pairs.

Resources from the Bible
(for optional use)

Self-Awareness
Romans 7:14-25 — 1 do the very things I don't want to do.
Galatians 5:22-23 — Fruit of the Spirit: love, joy, peace, patience, etc.

Self-Worth
Psalm 8 — "What is man . . .?"
Psalm 23 — The Lord is my Shepherd.
Psalm 100 — God made us: we are his people.
Isaiah 49:16 — God does not forget us.
Matthew 10:28-31 — God's love and the sparrows.
Luke 15:3-10 — The worth of each individual.
John 3:16 — God's love for the world.
John 14:1-4 — A place for us.
1 Corinthians 3:16-17 — Our body is God's temple.
1 John 3:1-3 — We are God's children.

Success; Happiness
Joshua 1:8 — Guidelines for "good success."
Ecclesiastes 5:19 — Enjoyment in work.
Matthew 5:1-11 — Beatitudes — a blessed life.
John 13:3-17 — Happiness is serving.
1 Timothy 6:6-10 — Secret of contentment.

Talents, Time, and Money
Romans 12:1-8 — Different gifts.
Matthew 6:25-33 — Concern for material things.
Mark 10:17-22; Luke 12:13-21 — Wealth and abundance can create obstacles.
Matthew 6:19-24 — The heart is where the treasure is.
Luke 12:48 — High expectations for some people.
Matthew 25:14-30 — Parable of the Talents.
Ephesians 5:15-17 — Responsible living and use of time.
Luke 6:38 — Generosity.
Mark 12:41-44 — The Widow's Mite — gave all she had.

2 Corinthians 8 and 9	Generous and cheerful giving.
Acts 20:35	Joy in giving.
1 Timothy 6:7; Matthew19:23-24	It isn't easy to be rich.
Genesis 28:22	A tenth to God.

Serving

Matthew 5:16	Giving God the glory.
Luke 10:25-28	Great commandment: Love God, love your neighbor as yourself.
Matthew 20:20-28	Key to true greatness.
2 Corinthians 3:2-3	People's lives are like letters.
Galatians 6:9	Service can be tiring.
1 Peter 5:2	Serve gladly — not grudgingly.

Life-style

Acts 2:44-47	Life-style of the early Church.
Acts 4:32-35	Everything in common.

Work, Leisure

Ecclesiastes 3	A time and a season for everything.
Ecclesiastes 3:10-22	Enjoyment in work is one of God's gifts.
2 Thessalonians 3:6-10	No work, no eat.

Prayer

Lord, I truly believe you created me — a marvelous, unique creation. I belong to you. Sometimes, this gift of life troubles me at the same time that it amazes me. Sometimes I become confused trying to live up to the expectations of others and yet wanting to be myself.

But your constant reminder is that I am yours, that you care about me just the way I am. Thank you for making me whole. I can be myself again — appreciating the worth, the beauty of your creation. Help me to be all that I might be, as a special part of that creation, so that I may add to your glory.

Valuing Others

How do we see other persons, especially those who are in need and who are hurting? What is our responsibility to them, to ourselves, and to our God? And how do we handle things when we are hurting and need others?

Christian teachings challenge people to live a life which reflects their love for God, their neighbor, and themselves. Jesus taught that these relationships are intertwined. He said that we should love our neighbor as ourselves. This love becomes a very part of our being. It is expressed in our everyday life and thought and in our interaction with other persons.

This section is intended to help people examine human relationships in the light of God's love and forgiveness. How much do we really care about others? How do we think, feel, and behave as human beings in relation to other human beings and as a part of God's total creation?

Before using this chapter, please review the chapter on leadership.

 ## Voting

Instructions: Pages 30-31 give purpose and procedure for the .a Voting exercise.

Participants vote in the following manner:

Agree?	(Raise hand.)
Strongly Agree?	(Wave hand.)
Disagree?	(Thumb down.)
Strongly Disagree?	(Shake thumb.)
Pass?	(Fold arms across chest.)

General Voting Questions on Valuing Others

How many of you:

- are disturbed because you don't know how to help people?
- find that recognizing one's own limitations makes a person more accepting of another's shortcomings?
- think listening to another person is one way of accepting him or her?
- think that modern conveniences have cut people off from one another?
- think too many people are indifferent to the world around them?
- think most people practice what they preach?
- think that sin is an unavoidable part of human nature?
- find it difficult to say you're sorry?
- think that people have unlimited rights over their bodies?
- think that self-concern causes ecological crises?
- think that poor people have a right to protest their circumstances?
- think men need liberating as well as women?

Helping Others

How many of you:

- willingly help others?
- think that people need each other's help in order to mature?
- ever received an unexpected kindness from someone?
- ever received help from a whole group of people?
- were ever refused when you requested help?
- feel obligated to someone who helps you?
- expect your favors to be returned?
- quickly defend someone who is being ridiculed?

- ever stood up for a person who was not present to defend himself or herself?
- think others suspect your motives when you try to help?
- would stop to help someone fix a flat tire?
- help people who are unable to repay you?
- think that gratitude for God's gift of life requires that we devote our life to serving others?
- think that new ideas in technology usually help relieve human needs?
- think that some oppressed people are worthy of help, but some are not?
- think we can't really help poor people unless we understand their oppression?
- think that by helping minority groups and the poor, we help ourselves?
- find it difficult to understand and really help people of the Third World?
- are bothered when the Church sends food and clothing to communist countries or to protesting minorities?
- think the poor should receive free medical care?
- think better housing should be available to those who need it but can't afford it?

Sharing
How many of you:

- think there is a limit to how much a person can bear of another's burdens?
- think the Church community does not share enough with one another?
- think our relationships in groups would be richer if we would rely more on God's Spirit?

Roland S. Larson & Doris E. Larson

- feel that sharing deeply with another person is often too risky?
- think some people are afraid to be free and open with you?
- have ever betrayed a confidence?
- know one or two persons who can really confide in you?
- have tried to share and be open but were turned away?
- have a close friendship with someone because you shared a troubled period of time together?
- think that if you take the Gospel seriously, you really need to share the suffering and joy of others?
- think that greed underlies all the world's problems?
- think that if we use our resources wisely, there's plenty for everyone.

Loving

How many of you:

- think all people are lovable in some way?
- know someone you really don't like?
- think we will know how to love others if we know God?
- think it's impossible to love everybody?
- think loving means, specifically, taking care of the needy?
- think we grow as persons when we love others as ourselves?
- think that the more deeply we love, the more deeply we feel pain?
- think that the more deeply we love, the more deeply we are alive?

Listening and Accepting

How many of you:

- sometimes wonder if you listen carefully enough to what others say?

- think listening to another person is one way of accepting him or her?

- are often concerned only with what you want to say in a conversation?

- think everyone has an idea worth listening to?

- ever felt that nobody was listening to you?

- sometimes feel angry with another person who monopolizes a conversation?

- accept people whose lifestyles differ greatly from yours?

- accept people whose lifestyles you consider "unproductive?"

- think that yours is the only true religion?

- ever dropped a friend because his or her ideas were incompatible with yours?

- think that if we do not fear and hate, we do not arouse fear and hatred in others?

- sometimes make snap judgments about people?

- became friends with someone you didn't think you would like?

- think that most people are influenced too much by the opinions of others?

- believe people of all races are similar but shouldn't mingle?

- would vote for the best-qualified presidential candidate regardless of his or her race?

- would feel O.K. about living next door to a person of another race?

- think that people of all races have basically the same needs?

- have had a person of another race in your home during the past year?
- would date a person of another race?
- think manual labor is inferior to intellectual pursuits?
- would not object to a "half-way house" for chemically dependent persons in your neighborhood?
- think we should be careful about allowing persons of certain religions into our country?
- are interested in learning about others with different religious beliefs from yours?

Reaching Out to Our Neighbors and Others
How many of you:
- have a good relationship with most of your neighbors?
- have neighbors who are friendly but are not your friends?
- have a neighbor you could depend on in an emergency?
- are usually one of the first in your area to meet a new neighbor?
- would probably be one of the last in your area to meet a new neighbor?
- wish your neighborhood had a "sense of community?"
- have ever wondered what your neighborhood would be like if all of you depended on one another?
- feel that sometimes neighbors intrude on each other?
- have ever been annoyed by an overly helpful neighbor?
- have tried to reach out to a lonely person in the last month?
- tried to reach out to another person and were rejected?

- think people in your generation don't seem to need one another as much as they did in your parents' generation?
- think that modern conveniences have cut people off from one another?
- wish people weren't so private?
- prefer privacy?
- find that it is difficult today to get to know people deeply?
- would like to reach out more to people?
- would rather have one or two close friends than many friends?
- spend time with older people and enjoy it?
- find it depressing to be with people who have many problems?
- avoid people who have problems?
- avoid contacts with the handicapped?
- enjoy contacts with the handicapped?

Taking a Stand and Being Responsible

How many of you:

- think your vote counts?
- think your ideas about most things count?
- would like to take a stand on an issue but don't have enough facts?
- would like to know more about what your pastor thinks about social issues such as war, abortion, drugs, etc.?
- find it difficult to defend an unpopular view before a group?
- have nevertheless defended such a view before a group?
- think it's a waste of time to worry about political issues?

- think you should be involved in political and social issues?
- have ever carried a picket sign?
- have ever publicly taken a stand on an issue?
- think that participation in a demonstration is sometimes a Christian duty?
- think that as long as you are law-abiding, you needn't show any other interest in government?
- think other people should be completely responsible for themselves?
- think each nation should determine its own socio-economic and political systems?
- concentrate more on the needs of others than on your own needs?
- think it is possible to care so much for others that we neglect ourselves?
- think the oppressed have a right to resort to violence to obtain their rights?
- worry about violence in cities?
- worry about starving people in the world?
- think that a person should mostly worry about himself or herself and let others fend for themselves?
- think most Christians are concerned about oppressed people?
- think a Christian has the responsibility to prevent an acquaintance from committing suicide?
- think social reformers, in emphasizing the reform, sometimes forget the people?
- think people often neglect their families in order to be involved in community and church life?
- think a Christian can expect to suffer some inconvenience or persecution?
- would be willing to take a cut in salary as a part of a long-range effort to feed the hungry?

How many of you agree with this statement?

- What you do is your own business as long as you don't harm others.
- Conversion to Christianity implies having a sense of responsibility for others.
- We are accountable for the choices we make.
- We are accountable for what our choices do to others.
- The Church has an obligation to speak up on social and political issues.
- The Church should spend more time, energy, and money serving people in prisons, nursing homes, and hospitals.

How many of you agree with this statement on population?

- Population growth in the United States is harmful to our economy.
- Fewer people means less pollution.
- The population problem is manageable and can be dealt with gradually over the years.
- The population explosion will lead to the end of the human race.
- Legislation should restrict the number of children per family.

How many of you agree with this statement on war?

- Nuclear warfare can never be justified, even if some other forms of war can.
- War is always wrong.
- Citizens should have more choice in whether they have to fight in a war.
- Christians should serve their country willingly in any war.
- Both sides lose in any war.

- Many Christians have changed their attitudes toward war in recent years.
- Traditional "conditions for a just war" cannot be defended today.

How many of you agree with this statement on women?

- Women should be allowed and encouraged to serve and hold office in all areas of the Church's life.
- The Church has made second-class citizens of women.
- Men need liberating as well as women.
- Jesus treated women as persons more than men do today.
- The Church should encourage women to enter all fields of human endeavor.
- Men are naturally superior to women in administrative positions.
- Women's insights are needed in such fields as theology and politics.
- Women are harming themselves by wanting equality with men.
- Marriage and family life can be as good or better if women enter more into fields where men now predominate.
- The government should help support day-care centers for the children of working mothers.

How many of you agree with this statement on unwanted pregnancy?

- Women have unlimited rights over their bodies.
- The unborn child should have the same rights as a child at birth.
- The Scriptures are clear on the morality of abortion.
- Abortion should be a medical decision between the pregnant woman and her doctor.

- There are psychological, social, or economic circumstances that justify abortion in some cases.
- Abortion is allowable as long as it is not used as a means of birth control.
- From the moment of conception, life is to be protected by all reasonable means.
- More understanding and help should be given to unwed mothers.
- In some situations, families should be encouraged to put a child out for adoption.
- More men should take responsibility for birth control by vasectomy.
- There would be fewer abortions if more help were given parents of unwanted children.
- The Church provides little help when a woman is faced with the dilemma of an unwanted pregnancy.

How many of you agree with this statement on the treatment of the terminally ill?

- A patient has the right to know of his or her terminal illness.
- Terminally-ill patients should have the right to determine how long their life will be prolonged.
- Life is a gift from God, and a person has no option to terminate it.
- It is possible to decide at what point being alive becomes meaningless.
- A terminally-ill person should be kept alive as long as possible by whatever means, regardless of whether there is hope of recovery.
- There is no moral obligation to use extraordinary means to preserve the life of a terminally-ill person who does not wish his or her life prolonged.

Sin and Forgiveness
How many of you agree with this statement?

- Defining the word "sin" is difficult.
- Sin is too strong a word.
- Sin and crime are the same.
- Stealing food for a starving child is wrong.
- Sin is basically separation from God.
- Sin is an unavoidable part of human nature.
- We are born sinful.
- Sin is basically selfishness.
- An act is either right or wrong; there is nothing in between.
- Telling a lie is always wrong.
- Sin always hurts someone.
- You sin against God when you wrong another person.
- Society often excuses sin by calling it "mental illness."
- Guilt feelings are a healthy deterrent to wrongdoing.
- Sex crimes should be dealt with more severely.

How many of you:

- have wondered what it would be like if there were no forgiveness?
- think human beings cannot completely forgive and forget?
- have been forgiven and felt a sense of relief?
- have ever forgiven someone who never found out about it?
- ever asked someone to forgive you?
- find it difficult to say you're sorry?
- have been deeply hurt by another person and then forgave that person?
- think forgiveness sometimes involves a promise in return?

- think most people have trouble practicing forgiveness?
- think there is something for which you could never forgive a person?
- know someone you cannot forgive?

Ecology and the Environment
How many of you agree with this statement?

- Increasing the gross national product increases the junk piles around us.
- Most Americans believe that the consumption of "things" makes people happy.
- We consume too much.
- We need to re-evaluate our lifestyles.
- Economic progress and protection of the environment are not compatible.
- The wealthy cause more pollution than the poor.
- Our country is the major polluter of the world.
- The world needs more technology.
- We need to humanize the technology that already exists.

How many of you:

- think we don't really appreciate and use the natural resources God created for us?
- think we must learn to live with nature rather than to control nature?
- think that concern for profit is the main cause of ecological crises?
- think that most industrialists are as concerned about pollution as environmentalists are?
- spend much time in the out-of-doors?
- would like to spend more time in nature but are too busy?
- are concerned about the use of land in America?

- have ever written a letter to a government official regarding the use and care of natural resources?
- feel we have ignored the wisdom of American Indians in matters of conservation?

How many of you:
- overspend?
- own two cars?
- save your glass bottles and cans for recycling?
- often walk instead of drive?
- feel you have more clothes than you need?
- think it's a good idea to increase auto registration fees with increased engine size?
- would be willing to ride in a car pool or take the bus regularly?
- could get along without a car? could get by with one car?
- would be willing to share major appliances such as freezers or lawn mowers with other neighbors?
- would feel lost if you had no TV?
- own an air conditioner?
- would consider communal living to reduce the use of land and appliances?

Ranking

Instructions: Pages 31-32 give purpose and procedure for the Ranking exercise.

Participants rank all items in order of preference or priority (1 = most important; 2 = next most important, etc.)

General Ranking

For me, the joy of being a Christian is:

____ knowing my sins are forgiven.

____ sharing in Christ's work by serving others.

____ sharing in fellowship with other Christians.

For me, the "Good News" of the Gospel is that there is:

____ a God who loves us.

____ freedom for the poor and oppressed.

____ new life for us as sinners.

____ life after death.

My faith helps me to see people:

____ as brothers and sisters in Christ.

____ as sinners.

____ as people who need my love and service.

For life together in my congregation it is most important:

____ to know each other as individuals.

____ to know God and his Word.

____ to know and respond to the needs of society.

Your teenage daughter is pregnant; what do you think would be best for her?

____ Place the child for adoption.

____ Have an abortion.

____ Keep the child.

____ Marry immediately.

What is the best way to be involved in life?

____ Spend free time helping others.

____ Develop one's self to the fullest potential.

____ Be friendly to everyone.

____ Join a group that helps others.

Which do you think Jesus would choose as most important for his followers to be concerned about? (Rank five.)

____ knowledge of the Bible

____ being active in one's church

____ feeding the hungry

____ housing for those without shelter

____ companionship for the lonely

____ developing one's own potential

____ working with others for the common good

____ converting the world to Christianity

Helping

Your friend has a problem and you want to help. In which situation do you think you would be most effective?

____ unwed daughter becomes pregnant

____ spouse is an alcoholic

____ parent is dying of cancer

____ parent is in a nursing home

____ child is taking drugs

Which is the most helpful to people in need?

____ church

____ family

____ welfare agency

____ psychiatry

In the parable of the Good Samaritan, the Samaritan took several risks in befriending another person. Which risk would concern you most in helping another person?

____ getting too involved

____ becoming a victim

____ interference with other plans

____ losing money

What do you think persons in trouble need most?

____ advice

____ understanding

____ God's Word

Accepting

What do you usually do when confronted with a person whose values are different from yours?

____ accept the person

____ accept his or her values

____ try to change the person

Homosexuals:

____ are immoral.

____ need understanding.

____ are sick.

____ are normal people.

What quality is most important to you in a friend (or substitute one of these: boyfriend girlfriend, child, mate, parent, pastor, etc.)? Rank each group of three.

____ dependability

____ honesty

____ generosity

____ self-confidence

____ fairness

____ sense of purpose

____ similar interests

____ same race

____ similar religious faith

____ intelligence

____ sense of humor

____ outgoing nature

____ charm

____ respect for opinions of others

____ responsibility

My faith helps me to accept others because:

____ Jesus says I should.

____ we are all sinners who have fallen short of the glory of God.

____ I believe that we are all equally children of God.

Reaching Out

How can we best enrich the lives of the aging?

_____ Keep them in touch with persons of all ages.

_____ Help them share their wealth of experience.

_____ Allow them to be themselves.

_____ Visit them often.

Which is most likely to cut people off from one another?

_____ mobility

_____ conveniences

_____ privacy

Loving

Love is ...

_____ helping

_____ risking

_____ forgiving

_____ accepting others

_____ sharing

_____ listening

Which definition of love is probably closest to what Jesus talked about?

_____ Creating the best possible conditions for developing the potential of other persons.

_____ Loving the Lord your God with all your heart, mind, soul, and your neighbor as yourself.

_____ Giving to another when you see him or her in need.

Sin and Forgiveness
When you think of the word sin, which is it most like? Rank each group of three.

_____ eating too much
_____ wasting money
_____ working on Sunday

_____ ruthlessly cutting down forests
_____ strip mining
_____ being cruel to animals

_____ premarital sex
_____ drug abuse
_____ alcohol abuse

_____ not keeping your word
_____ not keeping society's rules
_____ Ignoring people's needs

_____ separation from God
_____ disobeying God's commands
_____ following the flesh instead of the spirit

_____ hating your brother or sister
_____ making money your number one priority
_____ stealing a TV set

_____ divorce
_____ deceit
_____ abortion

_____ a temper tantrum

_____ a sulk

_____ a putdown

Which of the following is the most meaningful title for the story of the Prodigal Son? (Luke 15:11-24)

_____ "A Son Comes Home"

_____ "Three Prodigals"

_____ "A Loving, Forgiving Parent"

_____ "The Prodigal Son"

_____ other:

For your past mistakes, which is most difficult for you to accept?

_____ forgiveness of God

_____ forgiveness of others

_____ forgiveness of yourself

Which is forgiving most like?

_____ totally forgetting

_____ restoring a relationship

_____ taking a load off another's back

_____ not judging another's behavior

Which do you think best expresses reconciliation?

_____ "Let's get together and figure out what went wrong."

_____ "I told you so. But let's forget it."

_____ "I'll be here if you need me."

_____ "What you did doesn't matter to me."

Taking a Stand and Being Responsible
What do you consider the most important concerns facing our society today? (Rank five.)

_____ racism

_____ war

_____ drugs

_____ violence

_____ poverty

_____ dishonesty in government

_____ juvenile delinquency

_____ aging

_____ sexual promiscuity

_____ vandalism

_____ abortion

_____ death and dying

_____ women's rights

_____ hunger population control

_____ ecology

_____ other:

What would best bring about international peace?

_____ Examine why people fight.

_____ Examine what Jesus says about love and peace.

_____ Become acquainted with people from other countries.

_____ Study the history and effects of war on nations.

_____ Share our knowledge and wealth with other nations.

A woman in her late 40s raised several children and wants no more. What do you think she should do if she becomes pregnant?

_____ raise the child

_____ place the child for adoption

_____ have an abortion

What would be the best reason for permitting mercy killing if an eighty-seven-year-old person were dying from cancer?

____ to save the family money

____ to spare the person needless suffering

____ to save society expense

Which is worst?

____ killing in war mercy

____ killing capital punishment

____ fatality resulting from careless or drunk driving

In what order does a Christian rank these responsibilities?

____ self

____ family

____ others

Ecology and Environment

What do you see as the biggest underlying cause of environmental problems?

____ population growth

____ high consumption

____ profit-motivated systems

____ political leaders who fear to act on their beliefs

____ indifferent Church leaders

____ apathetic citizens

What modern convenience could you do without most easily?

____ paper towels

____ plastic bags

____ nonreturnable containers

What could the American people do that would best relieve the ecological crisis?

____ get along with less

____ curb population growth

____ do more recycling

Continuum

Instructions: Pages 32-33 give purpose and procedure for the Continuum exercise.

Participants choose that place on the continuum, between two opposite extremes, which most closely represents their personal viewpoint.

General Continuums

How do you view your relationship with people in positions of influence and power?

├─────────────────────────────────────┤

dependent upon   independent of

What do you usually do when you meet a person whose values are different from yours?

├─────────────────────────────────────┤

accept them   reject them

To what extent should poor people in your community be helped?

├─────────────────────────────────────┤

Give the shirt off your   Give them nothing. Let
back. Share everything   them work and earn for
you possess.   themselves.

How do you share thoughts with friends?

├─────────────────────────────────────┤

tell them everything   tell them nothing

Reaching Out
Whom do you trust?

|——————————————————————————|

everyone   no one

Which are you more like with potential friends?

|——————————————————————————|

I choose.   I am chosen.'

Taking a Stand and Being Responsible

Pow responsible do you think people are for their behavior?

|——————————————————————————|

An individual is totally   An individual is not
responsible.   personally responsible.

Do you think abortion is morally permissible?

|——————————————————————————|

any time   never

How necessary are wars?

|——————————————————————————|

Our greed and fighting   People have the freedom
instincts guarantee wars.   and intelligence to resolve
                                                   all differences.

How do you feel about preserving wilderness areas?

|——————————————————————————|

leave them untouched   open them up

Either/Or

Instructions: Pages 34-35 give purpose and procedure for the Either/Or exercise.

Participants select, between two choices, the option with which they most closely identify.

General Either/Or Exercises

Which are you more like?
> ask / tell
> think / act
> repair the old one / buy a new one
> feed the world / care for yourself
> pragmatist / idealist
> forgiving and forgetting / forgiving but not forgetting

Which is more important in a friend?
> openness / loyalty
> willingness to help / willingness to listen
> generosity / intelligence
> dependability / humor
> an outgoing nature / a private nature
> independence / stability
> tolerance / honesty

Which are your relationships with others more like?
> winter / spring
> basket of eggs / building blocks
> agony / ecstasy
> sand castle / fortress
> welcome mat / no trespassing
> cozy / rocky

Which should Christians be more concerned about?
> listening / telling
> opposing / supporting

giving money / giving time
teaching / learning
spiritual growth / social change

Which better illustrates sin?
gossiping / telling a lie
cheating on income tax / cheating in an exam
harmful thoughts / harmful deeds
harming oneself / harming another
abortion / child abuse
indifference / acts of revolt
misuse of power / misuse of knowledge

Which is more dehumanizing to people?
caste system / racial discrimination
cruel punishment / total neglect
active dislike / silence
prison system / lack of education
poverty / welfare
pornography / stereotyping

 # Listening

Instructions: Pages 35-37 give purpose and procedure for the Listening exercise.

Participants respond to a stimulus statement in groups of three. Each person is "on focus" for five minutes.

Sin and Forgiveness

Tim and Bob had these reactions to the story of the adulterous woman and Jesus' response to her in John 7:53-8:11.

Tim: "Jesus must have recognized the woman's strong sexual drive and felt bad about the trouble she was in. The way he handled the situation — with compassion and strength — probably kept her from committing adultery again."

Bob: "I don't agree with you. Jesus was understanding, all right, but I think he was too permissive. He hardly mentioned her sinfulness. I think she'd have been better off if He'd forced her to admit her guilt openly."

When asked about her views on homosexuality, Harriet said, "I consider homosexuality a sin, but God forgives all persons regardless of their sexual sins, so we should forgive them too."

Myra responded: "I get upset when people say that homosexuals are sinful or sick. It seems to me that one's unselfish commitment to another person is the important thing, not what society thinks. Why can't we consider homosexuals to be as unselfish and loving as other people? Why call homosexuality a sin at all?"

Taking a Stand and Being Responsible

Mary Ellen said, "I know what to do when there's a sick neighbor down the street or when there's a family in our church needing food. But when I hear about the millions who are starving, or some huge area of the world suffering from a natural disaster, then I'm stumped. Those people are my neighbors too, but I don't know how to respond. My contribution of money or clothes seems so meaningless. I think that the Church must become more socially active, that it must help shape the social conscience of society by giving its members an understanding of the problems and issues. Then Church members would be able to respond intelligently to make this a more humane world."

Louise told her husband, "I'm really bothered by the way the Church and the gospels keep telling us to take care of others, to love our neighbors as ourselves. It's hard enough just raising a family these days without worrying about others as well."

Colleen attended a congregational meeting of her church. One agenda item was world hunger, and the response of most people seemed less than enthusiastic for supporting this cause. In irritation Colleen rose to her feet and said, "Can you imagine half of the world being hungry and many starving — right this very minute? Here we are, you and 1, with more than we need while millions of people are in desperate need of food just to survive. It seems to me," Colleen continued, "that Jesus said, 'I was hungry and you gave me food; I was thirsty and you gave me drink.' If our congregation doesn't respond, we are downright disobedient, immoral!"

Karen responded, "You're an idealist, Colleen. We can't change the world. Besides, how do you know our help would ever reach those people? It would simply line the pockets of the few who control the power. Let's concentrate on helping the people in our own parish."

Bert said, "In my travels around the world I've noticed that material wealth isn't the goal many poor people reach for. They want dignity and identity — and they wouldn't trade that for a piece of property or for a lot of expensive possessions. When we judge the motives and life-styles of poor people, we ought to be sure it's not just from our own middle-class perspective."

Dilemma

Instructions: Pages 37-39 give purpose and procedure for the Dilemma exercise.

Participants respond to a dilemma situation, exploring alternatives and consequences and finally choosing their own best solution.

Reaching Out

In your church, you've noticed a family that is often alone and appears uninterested in everyone else. You've never met them and feel a bit shy and uncomfortable about approaching them because they seem so distant. Today, you notice the mother and her three young children attending the morning service alone. The woman looks like she is holding back tears.

What can you do? What might happen?

Ann has made friends with a new girl in her class. The new girl is shy and has a speech impediment, and some of the other students have made fun of her. But Ann likes her and wants her to get to know Sue, who is Ann's best friend. Ann calls Sue to see if the three of them can do something together on Saturday. Before she has a chance to ask, Sue says, "Hey, I'm glad it's just you and me getting together next Saturday. Your new friend, Linda, is kind of a drag."

What could Ann do? What might happen?

Helping

You are an avid golfer and play every Saturday. This Saturday you long to be out on the course, but your regular playing companions had other plans. Your neighbor comes to your door in real despair, asking if you have time to discuss a personal problem that has been brewing all month. You say, "Sure!" just then, the phone rings. It's your new boss who enthusiastically says, "Guess what! We've got reservations at the Club. I'll pick you up in ten minutes. O.K.?"

What can you do? What might happen?

A disheveled-looking person stops you on the street and asks you for a quarter to buy some coffee.

What could you do? What might happen?

An 18-year-old girl whose parents live next door to you has written to you in confidence from another city. Last month she had a big hassle with her parents and left home. She is expecting a child, and there is no possibility of marriage. She expresses feelings of loneliness, confusion, and fear. She pleads with you to tell nobody, but wants your advice on what to do.

What can you do? What might happen?

Andy's peers look down on him because he comes from a poor family, isn't very well educated, wears shabby clothes, and generally lacks social graces.

Today, in despair, Andy confides in you: "There really ain't any hope for me to be any different kind of person than I am. I'm stuck with me. I can't help it ... I'm made that way."

What can you do? What might happen?

Accepting

Your best friend just arrived, very pleased with a new outfit. You think the outfit looks baggy and drab. Your friend says, "I blew my whole paycheck on this outfit. How do you like it?"

What can you say or do right now? What might happen?

Your 16-year-old daughter, Lisa, is quite popular with the kids at school. She has told you about a boy she likes named Gene. (You have not met Gene, but have heard that he is very nice. However, you were a little uptight when you found out that Gene is of a different race and religious faith than your family.) Lisa says, "Gene asked me to go to the big school party next Saturday. I said I'd let him know tomorrow. Is it O.K. with you?"

What can you do? What might happen?

Taking a Stand and Being Responsible

You are 15 years old and live in an all-white suburban community. Your folks have always encouraged you to love and accept everyone. Last week an interracial couple moved into the house down the block. Tonight the husband called and asked if you could sit with their three children. You were happy to get the call, but when you told your mother, she said, "Honey, Dad and I don't want you to baby-sit over there. "

What could you do? What might happen?

Jan told her friends that she just met Vivian Davis, a woman running for Congress, and was impressed with how articulate and knowledgeable she seemed. One of her friends commented, "Maybe so, but no woman will get my vote."

What could Jan say? What might happen?

You feel your political views are your own business, so although you are registered with a party, others are not aware of which one. A friend in your church is running for office, backed by the opposing political party. The friend calls you on the phone and says, "May I use your name in my campaign?"

What could you do? What might happen?

You are 13 years old and your friends mean more to you than almost anything. Five of you are at a friend's house, and the parents are gone. One of the girls suddenly appears with an opened bottle of whiskey and quickly pours five small glasses. You really don't want any, but all of a sudden one friend holds out a glass to you and says, "You're not a baby, are you?"

What can you do? What might happen?

A married couple in their middle forties have almost finished raising a family of four children. Their youngest is in junior high school. The marital relationship has been strained throughout the years, partly because of the demands of child rearing, and the couple plan to be divorced. Today the wife learns that she is pregnant and is completely distraught.

What can she do? What might happen?

You are a passenger in another person's car. He stops to buy gas and pays for it with a ten-dollar bill. You notice that the attendant gives him change of almost eleven dollars. The driver sticks the money into his pocket and mumbles something about "a lousy mathematician."

What can you do? What might happen?

A doctor tells a colleague about an elderly patient in Room 210: "That woman is terminally ill and suffering a lot. Her husband is dead and she has very little money. Her only son, some 500 miles away, hasn't much either. I can keep her alive with modern medicine for several months at enormous expense to her son's family, but again today she pleaded that I let her die now."

What can the doctor do? What might happen?

Miscellaneous Exercises

The remaining exercises in this section are one of a kind. The purpose of each is to help participants further examine what they believe about others. Procedures are given for each.

Name Tag

The purpose of this exercise is to help people get acquainted and begin sharing with one another. (Time required: 10-15 minutes)

1. Pass out a 4 x 6 card and a small piece of masking tape to each person. Then give these directions:
   - In the center of the card, print your first name.
   - In the upper left-hand corner, write or draw a place you would like to visit.
   - In the upper right-hand corner, write or draw something you can do well.
   - In the lower left-hand corner, write or draw a belief or value you hold strongly.
   - In the lower right-hand corner, put the name or initials of a person who has had a strong, positive influence in your life.

2. Have participants attach masking tape to their card and wear it. (Remind them of their right to pass. They can omit everything but their name if they wish.)

3. Have participants spend a few minutes milling about the room, meeting as many people as they can and talking about one or two of the items on their name tags if they wish.

   Note: Hundreds of suggestions can be used for the Name Tag exercise. Certain ones might be especially appropriate for a particular group, and you may wish to write your own items. Here are additional suggestions to get you started:
   - Write one thing you'd like to see happen in this community (or church).
   - Write the name of a living person you greatly admire.
   - Write the name of an historical figure you admire.
   - Complete this sentence: "Church is a place in which I. . . ."
   - Write the name of a favorite teacher, coach, or youth worker.
   - Complete this sentence: "Our community is a place where. . . ."

How Do I Forgive?

This exercise is designed to help participants examine their attitudes about forgiveness in relation to the behavior of others. (Time required: 10-15 minutes)

1. Write the situations described below on a chalkboard.

2. Have participants read the situations. Have them choose the three persons they are *most willing* to forgive; then have them choose the three they are *least willing* to forgive.

3. Ask each participant to find a partner and talk about the following:

   - why they made the choices they did;

   - the person that bothers them most of all;

   - how God might see some of these situations.

Here are the people and the situations:

- *Mrs. Jones* steals food for her hungry family.

- *Billy* steals fifty cents from his father's wallet.

- Fifteen-year-old *Rita* shoplifts with a group of friends for kicks.

- Bartender *Louie* goes looting during a riot in the inner city.

- *Judy* requisitions small articles from the place where she works and takes them home for her personal use.

- *Jimmy* snatches a purse from an old lady who has just cashed her welfare check.

- *Mary* steals money from a wealthy home where she is baby-sitting.

- *Nancy* pads her expense account.

- *Mike* steals drugs to support his habit.

- Once again *Perry* steals your time — promises to meet you for lunch and doesn't show up.

What Is Sin?

1. Duplicate the following page and provide each participant with a copy.

2. Allow participants 3-4 minutes to read and rank the responses.

3. Have participants gather in groups of 3 and share their rankings. Option: You may wish to use this as a Listening exercise. (See Pages 35-37 for purpose and procedure.)

Margaret and Joan are in a church-school class which has been discussing the meaning of sin. They were assigned to talk with several members of their congregation to find out what some of the adults think about sin.

Here is what the owner of a small business said: "Sin is real and people sin by choice. We are free to commit good or evil. This God-given freedom makes us personally responsible for how our choices affect others. We hurt others when we sin.

A homemaker described sin in this way: "Sin, as I see it, is putting other things before God. Sin is separation from God. In other words, when we don't keep God's commandments or when worldly things take priority in our lives, that is sin."

An engineer had a different viewpoint: "I don't think there's anything such as sin. Wrong-doing can be traced to people's environment or upbringing. Some people live in such poverty that they're sometimes forced to steal, even kill, just to stay alive. Some children grow up never knowing what's right or wrong. I know a young boy who was recently caught stealing. His father is an alcoholic and his mother really doesn't love him. You can't tell me that boy is responsible for his stealing. Maybe he did wrong, but I don't call that sin."

Which response came closest to your understanding of sin? Rank them.

_____ business owner

_____ homemaker

_____ engineer

Permission is given to reproduce this page for family and group use.

Values Statements

1. Choose a content area: ecology, hunger, equal rights, war, etc., and select voting items from the Voting section of this chapter (or create your own voting items).

2. Write the word *agree* on a piece of paper. Write the words *strongly agree* on another, *disagree* on a third, and *strongly disagree* on a fourth.

3. Post the sheets of paper, one in each corner of the room.

4. Call people to the middle of the room before you read a voting item. Then read the item and ask participants to select the corner of the room which best reflects their reaction (agree, disagree, etc.).

5. As it seems appropriate, give time to talk in pairs.

6. Call all to the center of the room again and repeat the procedure.

7. Keep a record of people's responses to each item you use.

8. For a closing activity, ask volunteers to quickly complete the statement, "I learned. . . ."

Report Card

This exercise gives participants an opportunity to reflect on their attitudes and behaviors toward others, particularly on acceptance and forgiveness in their personal relationships. (Time required: 10-15 minutes)

1. Pass out paper and then give these instructions: "Working alone, consider what forgiveness means to you. Using your own definition of forgiveness, describe and grade yourself in the following areas:
   - forgiving others in your family
   - forgiving others outside of your family
   - specific acts of forgiveness you have performed
   - forgiving others and forgetting." Allow 5-8 minutes.
2. Have each participant find a partner and share "report cards" with each other, along with some of their thoughts and feelings. Ask: "Is there an area you want to improve on? Why not describe it and set a goal?" (See pages 42-45 for Goal Setting.)

Butterfly

This exercise uses the biblical story of the Prodigal Son to help participants focus on the topic of reconciliation, examining their own thoughts, feelings, and experiences in the light of human forgiveness and God's forgiveness. (Suggested time: 20 minutes)

1. Participants will be working in groups of 4. Beforehand, prepare one set of Butterfly Cards for each small group. Cards can be made by duplicating the following page, cutting, and assembling into sets of four cards each.
2. Read Luke 15:11-32 to the entire group.

3. Have participants gather in groups of 4. Give each group one set of cards.

4. Give these instructions: "Silently look at the cards. Think about how you would arrange them to tell the story of the Prodigal Son as you understand it. Use your imagination; there are no right or wrong answers. just visualize a story-telling sequence for the four cards." (Allow 1 or 2 minutes.) "Now, taking turns, each person arrange the cards and share why you chose your arrangement. When the last person has finished, consider these questions:

   • How do you think the older son who stayed home would have arranged the cards? Try it, put them in a sequence. Tell why.

   • How do you think the father would have arranged the cards? Share why.

   • Have you had a similar experience when you felt forgiven? Can you arrange the cards to describe it? If you wish, share something about that experience.

   • What does all of this say to you about God's forgiveness?"

5. Have participants reassemble into one large group and share their learnings and their insights into God's forgiveness.

Butterfly Cards

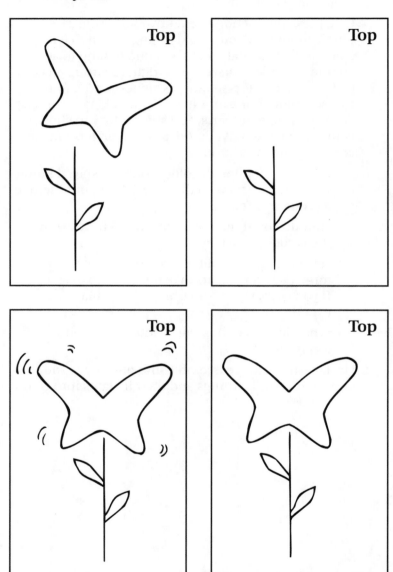

Forgiveness Discussion

(Suggested time: 20-25 minutes)

1. You may wish to write the questions below on a chalkboard. Then give these instructions: "Consider these questions one at a time. Jot down some notes on your responses. You will have a chance to share your reactions with others later on."

   - What is the first word you think of when you hear the word *forgiveness?* What does forgiveness mean to you?

   - If you were the Prodigal Son, would you have returned home? Why or why not?

   - If you were the father, how might you have responded to your son's return?

   - As you look at your life, are you more like the son who *left* home or the son who stayed home?

   - Think of times when you felt forgiven. What feelings did you experience? Jot them down.

   - Have you ever found it difficult to forgive another person? How do you deal with hurt and anger so that you are able to forgive another?

   - Have you known a situation where human forgiveness seemed almost as complete as God's?

2. Have participants share their responses in groups of 4.

Food Crisis

This exercise helps participants examine their feelings, attitudes, and values on the problem of hunger. (Time required: 30-40 minutes)

1. Have participants gather in small groups of 5 or 6 prior to giving instructions. Write the list of Food Users on the chalkboard. Then set up the situation: "World population is up; there was poor weather for growing crops again this year; the supply of food is down, and the back-up supply is down to approximately seven to ten days."

Roland S. Larson & Doris E. Larson

2. Give these instructions to the groups:

"You are members of the United States Commission on Food Use and Hunger. The immediate situation dictates that your group must plan to reduce food consumption in the United States by 25-30 percent. Your decisions will be implemented within sixty days.

"Your plan will probably be in effect for several years, as the situation is not expected to improve.

"During the past year your commission has worked on voluntary food saving plans. These have failed.

"Your task for today (you will have about 15 minutes) is to negotiate and decide which four of the food users must have their supply of available food cut drastically. If you have time, also designate four which you would be most reluctant to cut."

Food Users:

- restaurants, eating places
- American families
- friendly countries who need food, and are willing to pay two times the going rate for it
- hostile countries who need food, and are willing to pay three times the going rate for it
- producers of alcoholic beverages who require grain for their products
- hospitals, nursing homes, etc.
- people in the world who are starving
- needy persons in the United States (includes free school breakfasts in poverty areas, meals on wheels, etc.)
- schools, colleges, and agencies whose subsidized programs provide meals at reduced rates
- livestock, for meat production
- household pets

3. When most groups have finished, bring everyone together again. Ask groups to report:
   - whether or not they were able to reach a consensus
   - which areas they chose to be cut drastically
   - what values were behind their decisions

4. Ask participants if there is one thing they could do about hunger individually. Invite them to set a goal. (See pages 42-45 for Goal Setting.)

Thanksgiving Celebration

Thank List

(Time required: approximately 20-30 minutes)

1. Give these instructions to the group: "Think about positive things that have happened to you or are a part of your life today. Then list ten things you are thankful for." (Allow 5-10 minutes.)

2. Have participants look at their lists and ask that they do the following:
   - Star the three you are most thankful for.
   - Put an F by those things that involved your family.
   - Put a G by those things that involved your relationship with God in some direct way.
   - Put an 0 by the things that involved people outside your family.
   - Put an M by the things that largely involved money.

3. Ask participants to look over their completed Thank Lists and consider what they learned about the things they are thankful for.

4. Divide the total group into smaller groups of 4 people. Have them talk about their three starred items, those for which they are most thankful. Ask:

- What feelings do you have as you look over your list? Share them.

- Together can you think of a way to celebrate your thankfulness?

Three Levels of Learning

Give Me the Facts
Bible passages to read:

Two young persons named David and Jonathan had a close friendship. Read about them in 1 Samuel 20 and 1 Samuel 23:15-18, "… he loved him as he loved his own soul. And Jonathan went to David… and strengthened his hand in God."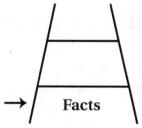

Naomi and Ruth, Naomi's daughter-in-law, had a beautiful relationship. See Ruth 1:16-17, "…entreat me not to leave you … where you go I will go…."

Jesus was comfortable with Mary, Martha, and Lazarus at their home in Bethany. He often stayed with them. One gets the feeling that each of them would be at home with the other(s). See Luke 10:38-42; John 11:1-44; and John 12:1-8.

What's the Idea?
Concepts to explore:

- What are the key aspects behind each of these friendships?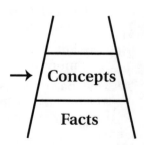

- Why are friendships important?

- What is meant by "Friendship is a gift?"

What's In It for Me?

Valuing suggestions:

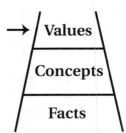

- Think of a person whose friend-ship has meant a lot to you. List that person's three or four most important characteristics which have enriched your relationship.

- In the total group, make a composite list on the chalkboard of all the personal qualities mentioned.

- To think about individually:

  Which qualities do you possess?

  Which would you like to strengthen, or add?

  Which characteristics would you value in a mate? Do you have those same qualities?

  Is there a specific goal you might set for your own growth in one or more of the desirable qualities?

Resources from the Bible

(for optional use)

Relationships

Matthew 5, 6, 7	Sermon on the Mount
Matthew 5:1-12	The Beatitudes
Matthew 7:12	The Golden Rule
Matthew 22:34-40	The Great Commandments
Luke 10:29-37	Parable of the Good Samaritan
John 15:12	Love one another.
Proverbs 17:17	A friend loves at all times.
Romans 12:9-21	Love everyone, including enemies.
Romans 14	On judging others. Supporting one another.
1 Corinthians 13	"…and the greatest of these is love."
Hebrews 13	Discipline in the Christian life.
1 Corinthians 12	Working together as one body.
1 John 3, 4	The love of God.
1 Thessalonians 5:11	So give encouragement to each other

Ephesians 6:5-9	Employer-worker relationships.
Malachi 3:5	
Ephesians 2:14	Christ brings people of different values together.
Philippians 4:8	"...fill your minds with..."
Galatians 6:1-5	Bearing one another's burdens.

Taking a Stand and Being Responsible

Genesis 4:1-9	Brother's keeper?
Jeremiah 26	A faithful prophet risks death.
1 Corinthians 10:24	Seek your neighbor's good.
1 John 3:17-24	Responding to a brother in need.
Daniel 1-6	Daniel took a stand.
Acts 6:8-15; 7:1-60	Stephen the martyr.
Acts, esp. 4:1-22; 5:27-33; 12:1-19; 16:16-40; 18:1-11; 22:1-27:44	Peter and Paul, courageous apostles.

Behavior and Forgiveness

1 Corinthians 6	The body is God's temple.
Romans 13:8-14	Love one another.
Galatians 5	Christian freedom.
1 John 2:9-10	Hate and love.
Psalm 51	David's cry for forgiveness.
1 John 1:9	Confession and forgiveness.
Luke 15:11-24	A forgiving father.
Matthew 5:21-26	Reconciliation comes first.
Matthew 6:14-15	If you forgive others
Matthew 18:23-35	Parable of the unforgiving servant.
Jeremiah 31:34	God forgives and forgets.

Social issues

Genesis 1	"And God saw that it was good...."
Genesis 1:26-28; 2:15	Care for the earth.
Job 38:4-7	"The morning stars sang together...."
Psalm 33:6-9	The word of the Lord and Creation.

Psalm 19	"The heavens are telling...."
Romans 8:19-21	Creation will be set free.
Revelation 21:1	"...a new heaven and a new earth."
Revelation 22:1-2	"...for the healing of the nations."
1 Peter 2:13-17;	Attitudes toward civil authority.
Romans13:1-7;	
Luke 12:11-12; 20:24-25	
Acts 5:27-29	"Obey God rather than men."
Isaiah 10:1-3	Injustice condemned.
Isaiah 58:6-7	A true fast: free the oppressed, share with the hungry and homeless.
Amos 5:21-24	"...but let justice roll down like waters."
Micah 6:8	"...justice ... kindness ... and walk humbly."
Galatians 3:26-28	"...neither Jew nor Greek, neither slave nor free, neither male nor female ... all one in Christ Jesus."

Prayer:

Lord, I hear you say, "Love your neighbor as yourself." I find it easy to love my friends and am grateful for each one of them. I need them; they are important to me. But I'm beginning to find out who my neighbor really is — the hungry, the lonely, the oppressed. There are so many in need. I want to love them — not just in word, but by doing something for them.

I need your courage and encouragement. Lord, teach me to accept your forgiveness in my own life. And help me to love myself so that I can reach out to others, loving them more fully and experiencing the joy of giving.

Valuing the Old and the New

People today are constantly challenged to examine tradition and change as these affect their own lives, their family life, and the life of the Church.

Christianity offers many resources which apply to our examination of the new and the old. And we think that the Christian faith is always a present reality, oriented to the past, the present, and the future.

Tradition and change can work side by side in harmony, or they can produce discord and divisiveness. Deep feelings are often involved as we examine our opinions, attitudes, beliefs, and values. Thus, it is most helpful if these exercises can be used in a climate of mutual respect, acceptance, understanding and love.

Before using this chapter, please review the chapter on leadership.

 ## Voting

Instructions: Pages 30-31 give purpose and procedure for the Voting exercise.

Participants vote in the following manner:

Agree?	(Raise hand.)
Strongly agree?	(Wave hand.)
Disagree?	(Thumb down.)
Strongly disagree?	(Shake thumb.)
Pass?	(Fold arms across chest.)

General Voting Questions on Old and New

How many of you agree with this statement?

- Change is O.K. if it doesn't happen too fast.
- The present is influenced by the past.
- Change just happens, and you have little or no control over it.
- Change is a fact of life-but a regrettable fact.
- Most people nowadays want too much change.
- The "good old days" were the best.
- Tradition is important, but change is important too.
- Change provides a chance for growth or renewal.
- It is practically impossible for a person to grow and change without having some feelings of discomfort.

How many of you:

- feel there's too much change in your life right now?
- have experienced growth through change in the last two years?
- have found by experience that old ways of doing things are usually better than new ways?
- have changed at least one traditional way of doing something in the past year?
- have changed jobs within the last year?
- think changing jobs is a risk?
- were nervous about moving from the lower grades to junior high or senior high?
- have changed an important belief within the last five years?
- have found it upsetting to move to a new place?
- have found it upsetting to try something new?
- have found change to be challenging?
- think God is active in change?

The Church and Change

How many of you:

- think people will support only that which they are a part of?
- think the Church should concern itself with all the current issues of society?
- think the Church has a great chance today to lead people into life-styles which are exciting and meaningful?
- think your own church is moving closer to the characteristics of the early Church?
- think there are many possible forms of church life in modern society?
- think most churches need to spend some time in squabbling and in argument?

How many of you agree with this statement?

- A good church-school teacher helps children think for themselves.
- Good church-school teachers should not try to make the pupil think and believe as they do.
- There is little hope for the Church's future unless pastors and congregations begin to communicate more.
- In thirty years your church body will unhesitatingly accept women as members of the clergy.
- A woman should be seriously considered as a senior pastor the next time your church has an opening.
- The bureaucracy of the Church often keeps people from the true Gospel and its meaning.
- If Jesus were a member of your church today, he would fit into your church life.
- The Christian church should encourage and support its traditions.

- Although many other things change, the Church should be the same yesterday, today, and forever.
- There is a sense of urgency to proclaim the Gospel in the Church today.
- Business organizations operate more efficiently than the Church.
- The Church doesn't set high enough standards for Christians today.
- The Church is a community of both saints and sinners.
- Most Christians do not really study the Bible and think through their faith.
- Most church members have lost the thrill of learning about their religion.
- The world sets the agenda for the Church.
- The Church sometimes establishes certain doctrines and practices which God never intended.
- A salesclerk can be carrying on a ministry as important as that of a pastor of a church.

Personal Reactions To Church
How many of you:

- feel protected in church?
- like stained-glass windows?
- like to pray in unison in church?
- sometimes fall asleep in church?
- wish your parents had accompanied you to church as a child?
- would want your own children to have the same kind of church life you had as a youngster?
- think most churches operate in a spirit of peace, love, and light?
- think that the local parish is an impersonal place?
- would be upset if organized religion did not exist?

Worship

How many of you agree with this statement?

- Worship can happen while you study.
- Worship can happen while you work.
- The Sunday morning service is really the only place of worship.
- Most people prefer simple hymns to chorales.
- The liturgy as we usually practice it is not meaningful.
- Group feedback after sermons would be helpful.
- Some of our worship meetings should be held in private homes.

How many of you:

- think your church listens when young people want to try something new?
- would like to be more involved in Sunday worship?
- would like new forms of worship?
- think the prayers in worship services are too long?
- wish the prayers in your church worship service were more personal?
- think your church's way of praying helps to create a worshipful atmosphere?
- can't relate to the prayers at Sunday worship?
- usually experience a feeling of joy in your worship services?
- think there needs to be a stronger relationship between church worship service and real life?
- habitually think of "other things" during the Sunday morning sermon?
- think that the effectiveness of a sermon depends primarily on the listener?
- cannot easily accept new forms in church worship such as contemporary music, dance, drama?
- feel uncomfortable with your present liturgy?

- would like to see contemporary worship used as an alternative form of worship?

- would like more hymn singing?

- prefer the old hymns?

- wish there were a wider variety of hymns sung during services?

- wish you knew more about the meaning behind Church symbols?

Holy Communion
How many of you agree with this statement?

- Before receiving Communion, a person should be certain of his or her worthiness.

- Everyone should be invited to receive Holy Communion.

- Children who have not completed confirmation should not be allowed to participate in Holy Communion.

- Only members of a congregation should be allowed to receive Communion with the congregation.

- Children should be encouraged to accompany their families to Communion and receive a blessing even if they do not receive the bread and wine.

- Lay people should share in distributing the bread and wine.

- The Communion liturgy should be very formal.

- The common cup should not be used.

- Communion is a joy-filled experience.

Ranking

Instructions: Pages 31-32 give purpose and procedure for the Ranking exercise.

Participants rank all items in order of preference or priority (1 = most important; 2 = next most important, etc.).

General Rankings on Old and New

If you were stranded alone on a deserted island, which would you rather have along?

____ the New Testament

____ the Old Testament

____ an anthology of great literature

____ an encyclopedia

Which is most effective in imparting values?

____ school

____ family

____ religious institutions

____ world leaders

Which most often happens when you experience change?

____ I'm stimulated to risk new things.

____ I feel more hopeful.

____ I ask more questions.

For life together in our congregation, it is most important:

____ to know each other as individuals.

____ to know God and his Word.

____ to know and be responsive to the needs of society.

How involved should your church be in the life of the outside community? Rank each group separately.

____ somewhat involved

____ heavily involved

____ slightly or not at all involved

____ The Church should keep a balance between evangelism and community building.

____ The Church's first emphasis should be on evangelism.

____ The Church's first emphasis should be on community building.

____ The Church's first duty is to be a servant to others.

Which would most likely happen in your church?

____ A black family would be welcomed as visitors.

____ A black family would be invited to join.

____ A black family would be ignored.

What changes are most needed in your church?

____ changes in facilities

____ changes in worship service

____ changes in education programs

____ changes in methods of community outreach

If Jesus looked at your church program, which do you think he would find most nearly fulfilling his goals for the church? (Rank each group of three.)

____ church school

____ youth groups

____ music

____ money-raising efforts for your own parish

____ giving to missions

____ membership pledges

_____ council meetings

_____ women's groups

_____ Sunday worship

Holy Communion

For whom should Communion be available?

_____ all those baptized

_____ only those baptized and confirmed

_____ anyone above ten years of age who is a believer

How often should your congregation receive Holy Communion?

_____ weekly

_____ monthly

_____ every three months

_____ oftener than weekly

How long should confirmation preparation last?

_____ one year

_____ two years

_____ three years

Church Worship

Which is of most importance to you in a worship service?

_____ experiencing a positive feeling

_____ being alone with God

_____ reaffirming faith in God

_____ feeling kinship with others

Which is the most important part of a worship experience for you?

_____ sermon

_____ music

_____ people

Which type of sermon is most effective at a morning worship?

____ One that challenges the intellect.

____ One that preaches the Gospel.

____ One that challenges me to reach out to others.

In sermons, which should be emphasized most?

____ repentance

____ Church teachings

____ forgiveness

Which is closest to your meaning of worship?

____ sharing

____ thanking

____ praising

____ listening

Which hymn do you prefer? (Rank each group of three.)

____ "One in the Spirit"
("They'll Know We Are Christians By Our Love")

____ "A Mighty Fortress"

____ "What a Friend We Have in Jesus"

____ "Mine Eyes Have Seen the Glory"
("Battle Hymn of the Republic")

____ "Beautiful Savior"

____ "Jesus Loves Me, This I Know"

____ "Kumbaya"

____ "Joy to the World"

____ "In the Garden"

Which season of the Church year do you relate to most?

____ Advent

____ Christmas

____ Lent

____ Easter

____ Pentecost

Which do you think is the most appropriate musical instrument for worship?

____ guitar

____ organ

____ violin

____ piano

Which kind of setting do you prefer for worship?

____ church

____ nature

____ home

Continuum

Instructions: Pages 32-33 give purpose and procedure for the Continuum exercise.

Participants choose that place on the continuum, between two opposite extremes, which most closely represents their personal viewpoint.

General Continuum Exercises

|———————————————————————————————|

Who should be members of a church council?

Youngsters — the majority of the council should be young people, including teenagers. Older adults inhibit change. The Church needs the idealism and energy of youth.

Oldsters — only older members should be allowed on the council. The Church needs their experience and maturity. Young people are too impulsive — they want to change everything.

Which best enhances one's own spiritual quest?

|———————————————————————————————|

Go it alone — a person today needs more time alone, in quiet meditation, to reflect on his or her spirituality.

Be with others — people today need more corporate life, freed *for* each other and freed *from* self-isolation, for mutual love and caring.

How do you relate to others at worship service?

|———————————————————————————————|

I stay apart. Worship is a private experience and involves just God and me.

I get together with others. An important part of worship is mingling with others and making people feel welcome.

How important are church facilities to the Christian life?

|————————————————————————————————————|

Our church should be large and beautiful to attract people. People want to feel reverence and awe. And our learning facilities should accommodate many children and young adults.

We don't need a building at all. There's no need to be enclosed to worship. We should seek out people and minister to them wherever they are.

How do you feel about sharing leadership in a church?

|————————————————————————————————————|

Enlarge the church staff and give them complete responsibility for all decisions. We want our church to run smoothly and efficiently.

Every lay person should be involved in all aspects of church life. Then we won't need a staff. We can handle everything ourselves, including the sermons.

How can people nurture their own Christian lives?

|————————————————————————————————————|

Only through worship, Bible study, and church-related activities.

Only through involvement with the many people "out there" who haven't yet been reached.

Should the national Church body take a stand on social issues?

|————————————————————————————————————|

Absolutely, on each and every issue! We should be united, for an individual's stand is meaningless.

Absolutely not! Never! Stands on social issues are personal. The Church can't possibly represent all its members.

Either/Or

Instructions: Pages 34-35 give purpose and procedure for the Either/Or exercise.

Participants select between two choices that option with which they most closely identify.

General Either/Or Exercises

With which do you more closely identify?

It is safe. / It is right.
individual spiritual growth / social change
social action / evangelism
Life is a journey. / Life is a destination.
Change is challenging. / Change is threatening.
hearing or reading theology / experiencing theology
future / present
satisfaction with the present / hope for the future

Which change is more difficult to adjust to?

moving to a new city / taking a new job
getting married / having children
separation from family / losing a job
a new school / a new house
a new church / new neighbors
a new pastor / new liturgy
a new form of worship / a new biblical interpretation
breaking a tradition / breaking a habit

Which do you prefer?

contemporary worship / traditional worship
chorales / Gospel hymns
group prayer / individual prayer
worship in church / worship in nature
worship in church / worship at home
singing in the choir / teaching Sunday school
sermons / group Bible study
piano music / organ music
working with youth / working with the elderly

church wedding / home wedding
baptism during church/ baptism after church
common cup for Communion / individual cups
children at services / separate worship for children
colorful banners/stained glass windows
formal liturgy / folk liturgy

Which is happening to the Church today?
It is breaking down. / It is breaking open.

Which is Holy Communion more like?
a fellowship dinner / lunch with a friend
celebrating / meditating
joyful / solemn

Regarding church attendance for confirmands, which is best?
required attendance / voluntary attendance ·

Which is worship more like?
ministering to others / our inward response to God

Listening

Instructions: Pages 35-37 give purpose and procedure for the Listening exercise.

Participants respond to a stimulus statement in groups of three. Each person is "on focus" for five minutes.

The Church and Change

Adele said: "We should appreciate the old in the Christian Church — there's so much good in it. Many traditions have taken centuries to develop and have stood the test of time. Many people find their roots in such traditions. Traditions give meaning to their Christian experience. Too many people today want change just for change's sake. Let's hold on to our good, old ways."

Mary Jane wrote to a friend, "Fear seems to dominate most of a young person's church life. The Ten Commandments always come first, with all of the 'Thou shalt not's.' That's why the Church is turning kids off. That's why you don't see kids around after the ninth or tenth grade."

When Larry read Mark 2:21-97 (new wineskins), he interpreted it to mean: "Staying young in mind is of utmost importance. You've got to be able to change and adapt. Creating something new is really necessary, because the old can always be improved. You shouldn't patch a sinking ship — let it sink and build a new one."

Congregational Life

Eric, a high school sophomore, said: "In most of the churches in our community, people don't really care about one another. They don't even get acquainted — only a lot of surface stuff. Our worship would draw us closer together if it provided feeling-level experiences, not just an intellectual trip. And we should have more group participation in deciding what kinds of church services to have and how to carry them out."

Tillie gave this Pitch to the Membership Committee of her church: "The church is not requiring enough of its members. Members should have to tithe; to attend church regularly; to serve in some capacity; to devote more of their time to the church. After all, Jesus said, 'If any man would come after me, let him deny himself and take up his cross and follow me.' If people can't measure up to those standards, they shouldn't be allowed to keep their church membership."

The Church and the Community at Large

Abraham Lincoln once said, "The only assurance of our nation's safety is to lay our foundations in morality and religion." More recently a businesswoman said to her friend, "Religious institutions are no longer as influential as they once were, and their lack of influence has contributed to a decline in our moral standards. We need to recover the kind of religion our predecessors practiced. Apparently the separation of Church and state was a mistake. Church and government should unite to raise our moral standards. We've got to reverse the present trend before it's too late."

Church council members Elmer and Dan were talking about new directions for the Church's mission program. Elmer said, "The essential work of the Church of Jesus Christ is the propagation of the Gospel truth. The fundamental job of Christians is to reach as many people as possible. We've already spent much money and time on unbelievers in this community, but few have been responsive. Now we should broaden our mission effort — like that verse says -'go into all the world.' Churches should greatly increase their budgets to support mission work in countries where people haven't even had a chance to hear the Word of God."

Worship

Greg said, "True worship needs to include the great prayers of the Church, written or spoken, in language that is dignified. The Sunday service music should be worshipful and bring the congregation closer to God. I like guitar music and informal prayers at home, but they have no place in a Sunday service, because they don't create an atmosphere for religious worship."

Sherrie said, "A friend of mine thinks that people are the most important part of attending church. She loves to be with others, singing and praying and enjoying their fellowship. But you can be with other people at home, at work, in the neighborhood — every place. At church you should concentrate on God and on your response to him. It's a time of getting closer to God in order to know him better. I attend church because God is there — not because people are there."

Interviewing

Instructions: Pages 39-43 give purpose and procedure for the Interviewing exercise.

A volunteer from among the participants is interviewed before the group.

Identify from your group a person who is either more traditional (likes things as they are; prefers things not to change), or a person who is more contemporary (likes new ways of doing things; finds change exciting).

Select appropriate questions from pages 40-41. In addition, you might want to consider these questions:

- How long have you attended church here?
- What are some activities you have enjoyed or been involved in?
- Do you think this church has changed since you have been here? How would you describe the changes?
- What is one good thing about tradition?
- What is one good thing about change?
- Can you describe the kind of worship service you enjoy most?
- What does worship mean to you?
- Some people say that the old is better than the new; others say the new is better than the old. What do you think?
- Weddings take various forms these days. Do you prefer any particular type or format?
- Do you have any other thoughts about change that I haven't asked you?

In addition to members of your group, you may wish to interview one or more of the following:

- a person who has recently made a decision to enter a new occupation.

- a youth who has recently been confirmed.
- your pastor, asking some questions about the new and the old.
- a college student.
- an elderly person who is active in the congregation.
- a youth from a family whose work requires that they move frequently.
- a person who works in an area of specialty that is constantly changing.
- a career counselor who helps other people deal with change.
- a person who has made a major change in some area of life.
- a new convert to the Christian faith.
- your parents, using the form on page 258.

Miscellaneous Exercises

The remaining exercises in this section are one of a kind. The purpose of each is to help participants further examine what they believe and value about the new and old in the Christian church. Procedures are given for each.

Reaching Out

1. Write this list on a chalkboard or large sheet of paper.

education	ethnic minorities
health	celebrations
food	economics
energy	family
work	community
prisons	housing
women	other

2. Have participants copy the list and check any items that they think your church should be more concerned about.

3. Ask participants to rank in order of importance those three items your church should be most concerned about.

4. Have participants share their responses in groups of four.

When You Were My Age Interview

"When I was your age . . ." always seems to be followed by a lecture. This exercise invites youth to question

adults, beginning with "When you were my age . . .," to get in touch with the past and to find out what was important to adults when they were younger.

1. Duplicate the form on the next page and provide a copy for each participant.

2. Have participants interview one or both parents, grandparents, or another adult, jotting responses on the form.

3. Ask participants to bring their completed form to the next session.

4. At the next session have participants review the responses made to their questions. Give these instructions: "From what you've learned in your interviews, write a short paragraph about each person you interviewed, summarizing what seemed to be most important to them when they were your age.

> *Option:* Have participants share their learnings in small groups or in the total group.

When You Were My Age
Permission is given to reproduce this form for group and family use.

What was your favorite thing to do after school?
What kind of house did you live in?
What kind of games did you play?
Did you have a pet? What?
What did you like to eat?
What scary experience did you have?
What was the most important thing you owned?
What did you like to daydream about?
What worried you most?
Did you have a favorite book? Which one?
Where did you go when you wanted to be alone?
What fun things did you do with your family?
Did you fight with your sister or brother?
Who was your best friend?
What did you do together?
What person influenced you most?
When you were in trouble, who helped you?

1st Person	2nd Person

Church Future

1. Write the following Ranking exercise on the board.

   For the future of the Christian Church, it is most important that its members:

   - accept responsibility for justice and peace.
   - seek healing and creative encounter.
   - explore new ways of witness to Christ.
   - release the full potential in every person.
   - grow in personal faith and discipline in commitment to the faith.

2. Have participants gather in groups of 4 and consider their local church — its location, facilities, staff, and members — in terms of the items fisted. Ask which items are already important, active ingredients in the life of their church.

3. Have each group member rank the items in terms of the needs of their local church. Then have each group reach a consensus on the two most important needs.

4. When the groups have reached a consensus, have them examine the two items and brainstorm ways to fill those needs. (Pages 38-39   gives the procedure for brainstorming.)

5. Have each group decide which are the best three solutions and rank those three. Ask: "Do you see one first step toward a goal you might set? A step that is realistic, believable, and achievable? What is it and how might you accomplish it? How about setting an action goal?" (Pages 42-45 gives procedure for Goal Setting.)

Examining Beliefs

1. Duplicate the following page and pass out copies to each participant.

2. Have individuals rank the items given.

3. When participants have completed their rankings, have them find partners and share their rankings and reasons for their rankings.

Optional sharing: Participants could react to these three items in groups of 3, following the procedures for the Listening exercise. (See pages 35-37)

Three lay persons were asked: "How important is it for people to examine what they believe?" Here is what each said:

- "God speaking through his Word is the authority. Examining various beliefs is a waste of time because God has already given us the answers. Discussing diverse ideas only waters down God's message."

- "God speaking through his Word is the authority. But he has given us minds to interpret the Scriptures and comes to people in different ways. We must take a firm stand on what God says but encourage the expression of diverse ideas so we can deal with them in the fight of God's Word and in the loving climate of Christian fellowship."

- "God speaking through his Word is the authority. But we must focus on the love and compassion which permeated all Jesus' relationships with others. If we loved our family, neighbors, and others as Jesus did, then we could trust ourselves to respond to them the way he would want us to."

Church Search

1. Duplicate the following page and pass out copies to each participant.

2. Have individuals rank the items from most to least attractive to them as prospective church members.

3. When rankings are completed, have participants gather in groups of three and give these instructions:

   - Each person share your ranking, without giving reasons at this point.

   - Now talk about some of the reasons behind your choices.

   - What feelings did you experience?

   - What are important attitudes, opinions, beliefs, and values behind your rankings?

   - Would you have preferred a fourth type of church? Can you describe it to your group?

You have just moved into a new city with your family. You've boiled your choice of churches down to three which are quite similar in membership and size. They appear to be equally committed to the Gospel, and each sees a strong congregational life as part of its mission. The respective pastors make these statements to you:

- Pastor A: "We want to grow quickly and respond to the needs of youth and young adults. Thus our worship services are contemporary, and changes often occur. You wouldn't recognize this place two years ago."

- Pastor B: "We've tried different kinds of services, but considerable strife occurred when we tried to change things too much. Consequently, our church is very much like it was twenty years ago. We plan to keep it that way, for we've learned that what we have now is the most effective."

- Pastor C: "Our church is becoming a house church. We don't have many meetings in our church. In fact, we're thinking of selling it. Our council and congregation would like to use most of the money for missions — both abroad and in our city. I plan to coordinate this program so that most of our fellowship and worship will be done in our members' homes."

Permission is given to reproduce this page for group and family use.

Dimensions of the Christian Church

1. Write the word *proclamation* on a large piece of paper. Write *faith* on another, *fellowship* on a third, and *service* on a fourth.

2. Post the sheets of paper, one in each corner of the room.

3. Have participants gather in the middle of the room and give these instructions: "In a moment you will be choosing, from four interwoven dimensions of the Christian church, the one you think the Church should be most concerned about. You will see that a key word is posted in each corner of the room. When you have made your choice, please move to that corner. Here are the four interwoven dimensions:

   - to proclaim God's message to people.

   - to encourage a personal faith centered in Christ.

   - to encourage fellowship in the life of the Holy Spirit.

   - to be of service to the Christian community and to the larger human community.

   "This might be a difficult choice since all of these may be important to you. But if you were to choose one, which would it be?" (Repeat the four items if necessary.)

4. Allow time for discussion.

Church Goals

One church council used this four-corner Voting exercise to begin thinking about its own goals. (See procedures 1-8 on page 200. They were asked if they agreed with the following statements:

- It's hard to make your true feelings known in most church groups and church activities.
- Concern for family programs in a church means that "singles" are ignored.
- Ours is a warm, friendly church.
- Church provides something for everyone if people search it out.
- Sunday morning coffee is a positive factor in promoting fellowship at our church.
- Our church needs more small groups within it, to meet individual needs.
- New members at our church are integrated quite readily into the mainstream of church life.
- There are lots of cliques at our church.
- Most people at our church go out of their way to make a new member feel welcome.
- On Sundays we should have one traditional service and one contemporary service.
- Youth should be encouraged to participate regularly in activities such as ushering and adult Bible study groups.
- Our church provides ample intellectual challenge for its members.
- Our church needs more fellowship suppers.

The Auction Barn

1. Duplicate the Auction Barn Form on the next pages. Pass out a copy to each participant.

2. Give these instructions: "Each of you represents a different church. You will have $4,000 with which to bid on the items you feel are most important for you and your fellow church members. You will be bidding competitively with each other. You will now have about five minutes to study the items and decide which ones you value most. Allot portions of the $4,000 and record the amounts in Column 1."

3. After 5 minutes, begin the auction. Go through the items one by one and award each to the highest bidder. Ask each person to keep track of the items he or she bid on, which ones he or she won, and the amount of money remaining after he or she won a bid. Nobody can spend more than $4,000. Persons failing to bid successfully on an item can reallocate their funds in Column 2 for bids on other items.

4. After the auction is completed, have participants gather in groups of 4-6 and share:

   - the items on which you made your two highest original bids and your reasons.

   - the values that he behind these choices.

5. Give these instructions to the entire group:

   - Individuals, share your learnings by completing one of these sentence beginnings:

     I learned . . .   I wonder . . .

     I think . . .   I was surprised . . .

   - Small groups, what values predominated in each of your groups? What issues were raised that you would like the total group to know about?

   - Assembly, is there an appropriate follow-up?

   - Any next steps? (Invite suggestions.)

Auction Barn Form

Permission is given to reproduce this form for group and family use.

1. Unlimited church budget for 3 years.

2. Ability of your church council to make only wise decisions for the next 5 years.

3. Assurance that the Christian faith is active in the fives of people in your community.

4. An opportunity to donate $100,000 to foreign mission programs

5. A magic formula which would make everyone responsive to God's Word.

6. Complete trust within your congregation.

7. Double your church staff.

8. A beautiful, functional church complete with the finest pipe organ, debt free.

9. Absolute wisdom for your decision-makers.

10. A perfect personal relationship for yourself with God.

11. Assurance that you will fully know the meaning of life.

12. A membership which is committed to giving ten percent of all gross income.

13. An openness and honesty formula with a lifetime effect for everyone.

14. Assurance that you will be personally involved in the church in ways that give you complete satisfaction in service.

15. The opportunity to spend a full month with the religious figure of your choice — anyone throughout history.

16. Listen-ears which enable all to hear each other's thoughts and feelings.

17. The ability to be the most effective Christian in your personal outreach.

18. Absolute assurance that you will have eternal life with God.

	You Original Buget	Your Revised Bid	Items You Won

Tornado

This exercise gives participants an opportunity to examine the entire life of their church, in the event that it were to be rebuilt. (Time required: at least an hour is recommended, and some groups may need considerably more time)

1. Have participants gather in groups of 6-8 prior to instructions.

2. Present this situation:

   "Your church congregation has recently received two shocks. First, you are without a pastor, because he resigned to accept a call at another church. Then last month a tornado completely destroyed the church building, the only structure owned by the congregation. Insurance coverage paid off the mortgage. Five hundred people remain on the membership rolls.

   "Your national church body has decided to fund your congregation as a three-year pilot project to begin a program from scratch. They have made it clear that all decisions are to be made by a laypersons' committee; they insist that this be a grass-roots effort, with all responsibility and authority kept at the local level. Their only mandate is that whatever you develop must promote, for you and your fellow parishioners, growth in the Christian life. Their gift is $600,000 over a three-year period ($200,000 each year). Thus you are able to commit $200,000 for the current year.

   "You are assembled today to begin your work. Your group is the committee. You have the opportunity for a completely fresh start, scrapping part or all of the past if you wish. All facets of church life need to be considered — goals, staffing, physical structures, program, etc. Your committee's task is to begin developing plans for this new venture, in your own way. Designate one person to keep careful notes on all specific decisions made by your group."

3. Allow 30-40 minutes for small-group discussion and decision making. Challenge individuals to practice really listening to one another, hearing everyone's ideas and feelings.

4. Ask the total assembly to share their decisions, one group at a time. Then have them consider:

   - Are there any common threads that run through the various group decisions?

   - What dominant values underlie the decisions?

   - What did your discussions tell you about where your own church is right now?

   - What are some of the strengths in your present program? (Do you wish to reaffirm and celebrate these in any ways?)

   - Are there some areas which need modifying, changing, adding to?

   - Do the words of Christ give you any ideas, any directions?

S. Have small groups reassemble and consider the following:

   - What might be the priority area for possible change?

   - What available resources can help bring about that change? (Have groups list the available resources.)

   - Are there any specific actions to take — as individuals, small group, total assembly, or congregation? (Have groups list them.)

   - Who will take responsibility for the first step?

6. Give the total assembly these instructions: "Without lengthy discussion, quickly share personal thoughts, feelings, observations, decisions, or actions to be taken."

7. *Optional: Pass* out copies of the Telegram Form on the next page and ask each participant to write a telegram urging an individual or group to take a specific action. Have volunteers read their telegrams to the group.

8. Give the group these questions to ponder on the way home:

- Think about your personal involvement during this entire exercise. What did you learn about yourself? What did you learn about how you interact with others? Did you listen? Were you listened to? How can the *Church best* encourage input from people like you?

TELEGRAM

To:

Message:

_____

(signed)

Permission, is given to reproduce this page for group and family use.

Mining for Gold

This exercise builds on the positive aspects of one's church-life experience and can lead to action that will strengthen and enhance it. (Time required: 25-35 minutes)

1. Have participants list five things in church life that bring them satisfaction or happiness and circle the two main ones.

2. Now have them list three things in church life that cause them some concern and circle the main one.

3. Ask participants to gather in groups of 4 and share their lists, considering the following from the first list:

   • the important things your church has given your group members.

   • ways you can acknowledge, give thanks, or celebrate these.

4. Then give the group these instructions: "Using your second fist, identify any common concerns within your group. Decide which main concern people like yourselves could conceivably do something about. Brainstorm possible solutions." (Page 38 gives the procedure for brainstorming.)

5. Have groups reach a consensus on the best possible solution. Invite them to set a goal within their group and draw up a contract to achieve that goal. (Pages 42-45 give the procedure for Goal Setting.)

Church Cup

This exercise helps participants think about their own church — what it is now and how it might be changed. You will need a Styrofoam cup and a pencil for each group of 5 or 6 people. (Time required: 15 minutes)

1. Ask participants to gather in small groups of 5 or 6 people.

2. Give each group one cup and one sharp pencil. Explain: "Let this cup represent your church. Without talking, do anything you wish with the cup to express your feelings on what your church should be. What values do you envision as most important for your church? Represent these nonverbally in your own way — drawing on the cup, filling it, writing on it, puncturing it. The beginning person takes a minute or two to respond, then passes the cup to the next person. Repeat until each has had a turn."

3. Have participants take turns within their groups, explaining how they changed the cup and what that change represents. Then allow time for small-group discussion.

4. Reassemble the entire group and invite participants to share meaningful happenings, insights, observations. Encourage free expression regarding unmet needs of your church and possible new directions.

Thank-You Telegram

1. Reproduce the form on page 273, and provide each participant with a copy.

2. Give these instructions: "Think about your church. (Pause.) Then think about positive experiences in your church life. Think of a person who has helped you deal with the meaning of your life or who has enriched your church experience. Send that person a Thank-You Telegram, using fifteen words or less. If you like, send more than one telegram."

3. Allow 4-5 minutes. Encourage volunteers to read their telegrams to the entire group.

Celebrating the Old and the New

Remembering the Old Year and Anticipating the New

The Church values celebration; just note the many seasons of the year it celebrates — Advent, Christmas, Easter, Pentecost, among others. The New Year is important too, and celebrating it suggests looking to the future and reflecting on the past. This exercise provides participants with a chance to examine the important things about the old year. (Time required: 20-25 minutes)

1. List the following items on newsprint or chalkboard. Allow time for individuals to work quietly and alone, completing each item.

   - things I like most to remember about last year
   - a positive change in me during the old year
   - one new thing I'd like to change for the new year
   - a hope for the new year
   - my goal during the next year

2. When participants have completed their lists, ask them to consider the following questions: "Do any of the things you listed relate to your religious faith? If so, in what way? How has your faith changed over the past year?"

3. Introduce Goal Setting. (Pages 42-45 give procedures.) Challenge individuals to set a goal for themselves, write it down, and sign it.

4. Ask each participant to find a partner and take ten minutes to share their thoughts and goals.

Three Levels of Learning

Give Me the Facts!

God called *Abraham* to pack his belongings and go to another country. (Genesis 11:31-32 and 12:1-9)

Christ called *Matthew* to leave his job as tax collector and said, "Follow me!" (Matthew 9:9-13 and Luke 5:27-32)

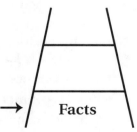

Christ confronted *Paul* in a vision and called him to change his ways. (Acts 9:1-22)
Questions to answer:

- Where did Abraham's family come from?
- What was his response to God's command and promise?
- What effect did Abraham's obedience to God's call have on him and on others? (Hebrews 11:8-19)
- By what name was Matthew also called?
- What was Matthew's response to Jesus' call?
- What special thing did Matthew do for Jesus?
- How had Paul been treating the disciples and Christians?
- What happened on the road to Damascus?
- How did Paul respond?
- Describe the events that followed. Who were the people involved?
- What was the result of the change in Paul's life?

What's the Idea?
Concepts to explore:

- What adjustments do you think Abraham and his family had to make in

---

- What problems confront a family moving to a new location within their country? To a foreign land?

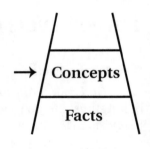

- What changes do you think Matthew encountered when he left his position as a tax collector to follow Jesus?

- Was a sacrifice involved? Explain.

- What is meant by the term "sacrifice?"

- What is a conversion? Does it last?

- Paul knew the time and place of his conversion. Is it always possible to know this? Explain.

- How can one explain the unquestioning, obedient response of each of these three men — Abraham, Matthew, and Paul — to a change in their life?

What's in It for Me?
Valuing suggestions:

1. Have participants take time to reflect on the following questions:

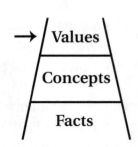

- What do the lives of Abraham, Matthew, and Paul say to you about responding to change? About coping with change?

- What feelings do you associate with change?

- Have you ever moved? What feelings and adjustments did you encounter?

- Have you known anyone who has sacrificed a good salary to take a new job that was more fulfilling than his or her present position?

Paul writes in 2 Corinthians 5:17 about the new and the old. "If anyone is in Christ, he is a new creation; the old has passed away, behold the new has come."

- What implications does this verse have for your life.?

- Have you known a person who made a major change in life-style like Paul did? If so, what sort of change?

2. Have participants share the following in pairs:

- Talk about any of the above that relates to your own life.

- Think about one change you have wanted to make to enrich your life — a change in a personal relationship, a job, a life-style, etc. What might you do to make the change? Discuss it with your partner.

- Consider setting a goal. Tell your partner specifically what you are going to change and how you will go about it.

3. Invite all participants to keep a list of the new and different experiences they have had recently, considering how those experiences have been meaningful.

Resources from the Bible
(for optional use)

Personal Change
Ezekiel 36:26	A new heart and a new spirit.
2 Corinthians 5:17	People can become a new creation.
John 3:3-4	"How can a grown man be born?"
Mark 1:18	Change of career.
Acts 9:1-22	A changed life.

Church
Proverbs 29:18	With no vision, the people perish.
Ephesians 3:14-21	Christ is at the center of the Church
Ephesians 4:13-16	Importance of unity — one body, one Spirit.
Romans 15:1-7	Encourage and help one another.
Philemon 1-7	Early house church.
1 John 3:19-24	God is truth.
1 John 4:7-12	Love one another.

Lay Involvement
Colossians 3:12-17	Life together in the Church.
Romans 12:1-2	God changes people.
John 8:31-32	Truth means freedom.
Galatians 3:28	All people are one in Christ Jesus.
Ephesians 1:3-15	A common faith, a common commitment.
1 Corinthians 12:4-6	Varieties of gifts, but same Spirit.
2 Timothy 2:15	Teaching — passing the Word along.
1 Peter 5:1-3	The importance of a good example.

Worship
John 4:19-24	True worship defined.
Psalm 95:5	A call to worship.
Hosea 6:6	The attitude in worship is important.
Matthew 4:10, 22:8	Revelation Worship focuses on God.
Luke 4:16	Jesus worshiped "as was his custom."

Jesus and Change

Matthew 5	Jesus suggests changed attitudes.
Mark 2:15-17	Ate with tax collectors.
Mark 2:23-28	Worked on the Sabbath.
Mark 3:1-5	Healed on the Sabbath.
Mark 2:18-22	New wine in old wineskins.

Prayer

You loved tradition, Lord, and yet you were always open to new things; you didn't let rules and old ways of doing things interfere with your love for people. Help me to be open to the beauty of the old and the challenge of the new so that I might be an effective person in your kingdom.

Bibliography

In addition to the Bible, you may find these books useful.

Augenstein, Leroy G. *Come, Let Us Play God.* New York: Harper & Row, Publishers, 1969.

Bach, Marcus. *Had You Been Born in Another Faith.* Engelwood Cliffs, N.J.: Prentice-Hall, Inc., 1973.

Becker, Ernest. *Denial of Death.* New York: The Free Press, 1973.

Bonhoeffer, Dietrich. *Cost of Discipleship.* 2d ed. New York: The Macmillan Company, 1967.

———. *Life Together.* Translated by J. W. Doberstein. New York: Harper & Row, Publishers, 1954.

Bovet, Theodor. *Handbook of Marriage.* rev. ed. Garden City, N.Y.: Doubleday & Company, Inc., 1969.

———. *Have Time and Be Free.* Atlanta: John Knox Press, 1964.

Brand, Eugene. *Rite Thing.* Minneapolis: Augsburg Publishing House, 1970.

Clinebell, Charlotte H., and Clinebell, Howard J., Jr. *Intimate Marriage.* New York: Harper & Row, Publishers, 1970.

Feucht, Oscar. *Family Relationships and the Church.* St. Louis: Concordia Publishing House, 1971.

Fowler, James. "Religious Socialization: The Faith Development Perspective." Paper presented at annual meeting of Religious Research Association, October 1975.

Frankl, Viktor E. *Man's Search for Meaning.* rev. ed. Boston: Beacon Press, 1963.

Freire, Paulo. *Pedagogy of the Oppressed.* Translated by Myra B. Ramos. New York: Herder/The Seabury Press, 1971.

Gelatt, H. B.; Varenhorst, B.; and Carey, R. *Deciding: A Decision-Making Program For Students.* New York: College Entrance Examination Board, 1972.

Ginott, Haim G. *Between Parent and Child.* New York: Avon Books, 1969.

————. *Between Parent and Teenager.* New York: Avon Books, 1971.

Glashagel, Jerry. *Valuing Families.* Youth Values Project. New York: National YMCA Board, 1975.

Gordon, Thomas. *Parent Effectiveness Training: The No-Lose Program for Raising Responsible Children.* New York: Peter H. Wyden, Inc., 1970.

Harmin, Merrill; Kirschenbaum, Howard; and Simon, Sidney B. *Clarifying Values Through Subject Matter.* Minneapolis: Winston Press, Inc., 1973.

Howe, Reuel L. *Miracle of Dialogue.* New York: The Seabury Press, Inc., 1963.

Hudnut, Robert K. *Sleeping Giant. Arousing Church Power in America.* New York: Harper & Row, Publishers, 1971.

Jourard, Sidney M. *Transparent Self.* 2d ed. New York: Van Nostrand Reinhold Company, 1971.

Kirschenbaum, Howard, and Simon, Sidney B., eds. *Readings in Values Clarification.* Minneapolis: Winston Press, Inc., 1973.

Kohlberg, Lawrence. "The Child as a Moral Philosopher." *Psychology Today,* September 1968.

Lewis, C. S. *Chronicles of Narnia.* 7 paperback volumes for children and adults. New York: The Macmillan Company, n.d.

————. *A Grief Observed.* New York: The Seabury Press, Inc., 1963.

————. *Mere Christianity.* New York: The Macmillan Company, 1953.

Menninger, Karl, M.D. *Whatever Became of Sin?* New York: Hawthorn Books, Inc., 1973.

Miller, Keith. *Second Touch.* 2d ed. Waco, Tex.: Word Books, Inc., 1972.

————. *Taste of New Wine.* Waco, Tex.: Word Books, Inc., 1965.

Mooneyham, W. Stanley. *What Do You Say To a Hungry World?* Waco, Tex.: Word Books, Inc., 1975.

O'Connor, Elizabeth. *Eighth Day of Creation: Gifts and Creativity.* Waco, Tex.: Word Books, Inc., 1971.

———. *Our Many Selves.* New York: Harper & Row, Publishers, 1971.

Olsson, Karl. *Finding Your Self in the Bible.* Minneapolis: Augsburg Publishing House, 1974.

Paulson, Wayne. *Deciding for Myself. A Values-Clarification Series.* Minneapolis: Winston Press, Inc., 1974.

Phillips, John B. *Your God Is Too Small.* New York: The Macmillan Company, 1961.

Raths, L. E.; Harmin, Merrill; and Simon, Sidney B. *Values and Teaching.* Columbus, Oh.: Charles E. Merrill Publishing Company, 1967.

Satir, Virginia. *Peoplemaking.* Palo Alto, Calif.: Science and Behavior Books, Inc., 1972.

Simon, Arthur. *Faces of Poverty.* New York: The Macmillan Company, 1968.

Simon, Sidney B.; Howe, Leland; and Kirschenbaum, Howard. *Values Clarification: A Handbook of Practical Strategies for Teachers and Students.* New York: Hart Publishing Company, 1972.

Smith, JoAnn Kelley. *Free Fall.* Valley Forge, Penn.: Judson Press, 1975.

Strommen, Merton P. *Five Cries of Youth.* New York: Harper & Row, Publishers, 1974.

Tournier, Paul. *Meaning of Persons.* New York: Harper & Row, Publishers, 1957.

Trexler, Edgar R., ed. *Creative Congregations.* Nashville: Abingdon Press, 1972.

Trueblood, Elton. A *Place to Stand.* New York: Harper & Row, Publishers, 1969.

Westerhoff, John G., 3rd. *Values for Tomorrow's Children.* Philadelphia: United Church Press, 1970.

Winter, Gibson. *Love and Conflict: New Patterns in Family Life.* Garden City, N.Y.: Doubleday & Company, Inc., 1958.

———. *The New Creation as Metropolis.* New York: The Macmillan Company, 1963.

Wold, Margaret. *The Shalom Woman.* Minneapolis: Augsburg Publishing House, 1974.

Zdenek, Marilee, and Champion, Marge. *Catch the New Wind.* Waco, Tex.: Word Books, Inc., 1972.

Additional Titles

Clarke, Jean Illsley. *Self-Esteem: A Family Affair.* Minneapolis: Winston Press, Inc., 1978.

Larson, Roland S. and Doris E. I *Need to Have You Know Me, A Guide to a Better Marriage.* Minneapolis: Winston Press, Inc.. 1979.

YOUTH & FAMILY
I·N·S·T·I·T·U·T·E
*A*UGSBURG *of* COLLEGE

Mission

The Youth and Family Institute of Augsburg College promotes the nurturing of healthy and faithful children, youth, and families who are committed to Christ and a life of service in God's world by....

1. Offering new VISIONS and MODELS for ministry with children, youth, and their families.

2. Training VOLUNTEERS and PROFESSIONALS in children's, youth, and family ministry.

3. Providing CONSULTATION and RESOURCES to individuals, families, and congregations of the Christian faith nationally and internationally.

For more information about the Institute or a catalog of resources please call (612) 330-1624.

Other Resources for Nurturing Faith and Teaching Values by the Youth and Family Institute of Augsburg College

FaithTalk

A set of 192 share cards to be used by families or small. groups for beginning conversations of faith and life issues. It is for children over 10 years of age and their parents or other caring adults to tell the stories of God's presence in their lives. The handy canvas carrying case holds 48 share cards in each of four areas: Memories, Etchings, Values, and Actions and is designed to fit in the glove compartment of the car, in a purse, or on the family table.

FaithTalk with Children

A set of 96 share cards, 24 in each of four categories: Memories, Feelings & Actions, Wonder, Growing Together. This resource was designed to be used by parents and other adults in conversation with children ages 3-10. It also comes in a canvas carrying case.

Scripture Talk

This handy spiral-bound booklet contains Scripture passages from both the Old and New Testament and a series of conversation starter questions for families and small groups to share how this Scripture applies to their lives.

Passages and Pathways

This resource contains lessons for small groups of parents of preschool children to support one another in their parenting. Seven areas of parental concerns are addressed: child care, rest and nutrition, toilet training, conflict resolution, happiness, television, grief and loss.